THE REVISED VERSION
EDITED FOR THE USE OF SCHOOLS

THE

SECOND BOOK OF SAMUEL

THE
SECOND BOOK OF SAMUEL

EDITED BY

R. O. HUTCHINSON, M.A.

VICAR OF ST SAMPSON WITH HOLY TRINITY, YORK
AND VICAR-CHORAL OF YORK MINSTER

CAMBRIDGE
AT THE UNIVERSITY PRESS
1911

CAMBRIDGE
UNIVERSITY PRESS

University Printing House, Cambridge CB2 8BS, United Kingdom

Published in the United States of America by Cambridge University Press, New York

Cambridge University Press is part of the University of Cambridge.

It furthers the University's mission by disseminating knowledge in the pursuit of education, learning and research at the highest international levels of excellence.

www.cambridge.org
Information on this title: www.cambridge.org/9781107647961

© Cambridge University Press 1911

First published 1911
First paperback edition 2014

A catalogue record for this publication is available from the British Library

ISBN 978-1-107-64796-1 Paperback

PREFACE BY THE GENERAL EDITOR
FOR THE OLD TESTAMENT

THE aim of this series of commentaries is to explain the Revised Version for young students, and at the same time to present, in a simple form, the main results of the best scholarship of the day.

The General Editor has confined himself to supervision and suggestion. The writer is, in each case, responsible for the opinions expressed and for the treatment of particular passages.

A. H. MᶜNEILE.

July, 1911.

CONTENTS

MAP

Available for download in colour from www.cambridge.org/9781107647961

INTRODUCTION

I. The Second Book of Samuel.

The Title.

THE two books of Samuel were originally one. We do not know who the author was. It could not have been Samuel, since most of the events happened after his death. They are however about Samuel, and the fulfilment of his work by David. It is the story of the rise of Israel from a low depth of weakness and subjection, to its greatest height of power and prosperity. The birth of the national spirit, which enabled Israel to form itself into a kingdom and free itself from the Philistines, was the result of a religious revival, begun by Samuel and the early prophets, carried on for a time by Saul, and completed by David.

How the Book was written.

It is a compilation from several documents. Most of these are very ancient. Chs. ix.–xx. are so full of vivid and living detail that we may consider them written by an eyewitness. To these extracts from other old records were added. In later ages fresh material was gathered ; sometimes expressions were altered to suit more modern ideas. It was not till after the Exile that the book reached its present form. Its growth had taken perhaps about 600 years. It must be noticed that the compiler joined his documents together with little adaptation Sometimes there are two accounts of the same event which do not always quite agree. (See notes on i. 6, x. 15.)

H.   *b*

The Purpose of the Author.

The author was a prophet, or religious teacher, rather than a historian. He taught God's nature and will by shewing what He had said and done to men in the past. The section of the Old Testament to which Samuel belongs is called 'The Former Prophets.' It is prophecy teaching by history, or illustration. Our book contains history, but as a history of David's reign it is meagre. On the other hand it is full of priceless religious lessons (see pp. xx.–xxii.), and describes fully those events which throw light on Jehovah's dealings with David and Israel.

II. ISRAEL IN THE DAYS OF DAVID.

Political Conditions.

(a) *Internal.* Israel was a small state consisting of twelve kindred tribes. Their bond of union was their common religion, the worship of Jehovah. Saul was the first leader who was acknowledged by all, but the tribes were still jealous and independent. The government of the chiefs ('sheikhs') gave way slowly to the authority of the king. There was strong jealousy between Judah, David's tribe, and the northern tribes, under the leadership of Saul's tribe, Benjamin. Those east of the Jordan were less excited by these feuds and more conservative. David, by a triumph of his wonderful personality, consolidated these elements into a nation; but in the reign of his grandson, Rehoboam, the north again parted from the south. The royal power in conflict with tribal jealousies, and the independence of great chiefs, are the key to the internal politics of this period.

(b) *Foreign.* Israel was placed among several small states, of race and customs similar to its own ; Edomites on the south, Moabites on the south-east, Ammonites on the east, and Syrians on the north-east. There were also Philistines on the west, and Phoenicians on the north-west. Some heathen clans still lived in Israel, such as the Gibeonites in Benjamin, and the Jebusites in Jebus, which was first captured by David. The relations of these people with Israel were friendly, when they were not at war. Israelites sometimes resided in Philistia or Moab. Foreign soldiers formed David's body-guard. The leadership among these states of Palestine was held by the Philistines, until David wrested it from them.

At David's accession the power of Israel was at its lowest; her armies were beaten; her territory was largely occupied by the Philistines ; her strength was dissipated by civil war.

(c) *The kingship.* Tribal government gave way to kingly authority, when Saul became king. But the chiefs retained considerable power. They elected the king. Abner made Ishbosheth king of Israel : David was elected, first by the Judaean chiefs, afterwards by the chiefs of Israel. He was not an absolute monarch. He made a compact with them at his election. He could be opposed and even checked by a powerful noble like Joab. Public opinion and ancient custom also limited the exercise of his will.

The kingship was elective, but it tended to become hereditary, since the royal family naturally grew richer, more numerous, and more powerful than other families. In Judah the kingship remained in David's family.

(d) *The royal tribe.* Tribal jealousy culminated in the feud between Saul's tribe, Benjamin, and Judah, David's tribe. Benjamites like Shimei and Sheba were fanatically hostile to David. Judah however considered that David did not sufficiently favour his own tribe (see on xix. 11 ff.). He offended his clansmen by moving his capital from Hebron, the tribal capital, to Jerusalem. Hebron afterwards was the starting-point of Absalom's revolt. After the suppression of that rising, David evidently pacified Judah by conceding them further privileges (xix. 11 ff.).

(*e*) *The army.* The king was commander-in-chief. Saul usually led his troops in person. David, after being constrained by his men not to risk his life, left the actual command to Joab, except on special occasions (xii. 27 ff.). A foreign corps, the Cherethites and Pelethites, guarded his person. He instituted two orders of chivalry for knights of special fame, the Three and the Thirty. A militia was enrolled as occasion required. His attempt to organise a standing army (xxiv.) was not successful.

(*f*) *Justice.* The king was also chief judge. To gain access to his presence the influence of an official was usually necessary (cf. xiv. 2). Absalom implied that imperfect provision was made for the hearing of cases (xv. 2 ff. n.). It was sometimes administered in a rough and ready way. David's award between Ziba and Mephibosheth is an instance (xvi. 3 f. and xix. 25 ff.).

(*g*) *Administration.* Saul's royalty had been of primitive simplicity. David organised a Court and a Government. He strengthened his own position by many marriages. He established a royal Shrine in Zion, where he placed the Ark. Close by was the royal palace and the barracks for his guards. He appointed officials, civil, military and religious (viii. 15 ff.).

Religious and Social Ideas.

(1) *The idea of God.* The revelation of God came very gradually. So we do not expect to find, 1000 years before the full light of Christ, the same knowledge of God that we possess. Some of the ideas of the Israelites were the same as those held by the other nations. They still thought that each land had its own god, who was the king of its people and fought its battles. 'Jehovah

of Hosts' was the leader of Israel's armies, as Chemosh was of Moab's. The Ark, the Symbol of His Presence, went with the hosts to war. The army escorted the Ark of the War-God to Zion. Jehovah shewed His anger by sending disaster ; His pleasure by temporal blessing. His displeasure might be averted by sacrifice. He abhorred a breach of covenant. In one important respect Jehovah differed from other gods ; He was a Holy God, requiring holiness in His worshippers. This was realised by such men as Moses, Samuel and David. But many still thought that so long as His rites were duly observed, He cared little about moral purity.

(2) *Means of revelation.* One way of finding out God's will was by the *Ephod*, a method of casting lots (see note on ii. 1).

Doubtless *traditional laws* had been handed down from Mosaic times, embodying an earlier revelation of God's will and nature, but the Pentateuch, as we have it, did not exist in David's time.

The record of *God's past dealings* with Israel, and *David's own experience* of His justice and mercy, also threw light upon the Divine ways.

It was a period of great *prophetic activity.* Some prophets were wild enthusiasts who whirled and shouted, as dervishes still do in the East. Some, called ' Seers,' gave oracles in a state of trance. Others, as Samuel and Nathan, were inspired to reveal fresh truths about Jehovah, to foretell the future, and to rebuke sin.

(3) *Worship.* Here too the advance from heathenism to the inspired ritual of later Judaism was gradual. In David's time Israelite worship was still in many ways like that of their neighbours. The Presence of Jehovah was localised at certain spots. Before the Ark (' before the Lord ') David danced and sacrificed. *High places,* where God was worshipped, had probably been shrines before the Israelites took possession of them. Jerusalem

became the home of the Ark. Hebron, Gibeon and Olivet were still reverenced as special seats of Deity.

The recognised method of worship was *sacrifice*. The ancient notion was that God and His people feasted together, and so became more at one. The blood, and in later times the fat, were the portion of the Deity. Sacrifices were occasions of public rejoicing and hospitality. Beef and mutton were eaten only at sacrificial feasts. Usually the sacrifice was offered by a priest, consecrated to the holy work.

(4) *The theocratic king.* Kingship was a religious office. David, chosen as he was by God, anointed by the prophet Samuel during Saul's lifetime, the hope of the party of national reform, regarded himself as God's vicegerent, sent to rule in God's name over God's people. He succeeded so far as he was guided by God's will shewn by oracles and prophets. He realised, as no other did, what Israel's king should be. He is therefore to later ages the ideal theocratic king, and the type of the Messiah.

(5) *The future life.* Death was a dark mystery, before Jesus Christ 'brought life and immortality to light.' There is no word of a future life in David's Dirge (ch. i.). Yet they did not think of the dead as annihilated. Samuel might return to warn Saul (1 Sam. xxviii.), and David spoke of going to his dead child (see note on xii. 23). They thought God cared for the wellbeing and permanence of the nation or tribe, rather than of the individual. Perpetuity for David's house is promised (vii. 12 f.), not immortality for himself.

(6) *The blood-feud.* This was one of the most stringently observed customs. In primitive society it was the chief safeguard of life. A man hesitated to shed the blood of one belonging to another clan, when he knew that every clansman of the dead man would consider it a sacred duty to avenge it. The tie of blood was the

strongest known. According to this code, Joab was right in slaying Abner for Asahel's death ; David, being of the same clan, was wrong in letting him go. But this rough justice was repugnant to David's higher ideal of government and belief in God's mercy.

(7) *War*. Every war was to the Israelites a holy war. Jehovah went before His hosts, to take part as their champion in 'the wars of the Lord' against 'the enemies of the Lord.' Warriors were consecrated men. When on active service they could not enter their homes, sleep in beds, nor go about ordinary work (see xi. 11, note on xxiv. 1).

(8) *The ban*. A conquered nation was often consecrated to Jehovah, i.e. destroyed utterly. Joshua destroyed Jericho, and Saul was sent to annihilate Amalek. In David's time less fierce views were held. With the Philistines and Jebusites he cultivated friendly relations. The Ammonites he apparently reduced to slavery and forced labour at his buildings. Only against Edom (1 Kings xi. 15 f.) and Moab (partially) did he execute the ban. These may have shewn some special hatred against Israel in her weakness.

III. The Life and Character of David.

(1) The early part of David's life, as shepherd, courtier, warrior and exile is told in 1 Samuel. During that period he was trained for his future work. As Saul's commander, and still more as chief of freebooters, he acquired his wonderful skill in managing men. During the period of his exile, his camp of outlaws seems to have been the real centre of law and order in Israel.

(2) After Saul's death, Abner and Ishbosheth, Saul's only surviving son, fled to Mahanaim in Gilead, where Ishbosheth was proclaimed king.

David, meanwhile, was elected king of Judah in Hebron. This was his first step towards the kingship, to which Samuel had anointed him. He sent a friendly messenger to the Gileadites announcing his accession and calling them to join him. For the time however Northern and Eastern Israel acknowledged Ishbosheth.

The position of the latter was precarious. He probably had to make humiliating terms with the victorious Philistines; while Ammon and Moab were hostile and aggressive neighbours. A strong party among his followers was for uniting the kingdom under David. His claims and those of David were certain to clash. A battle took place at Gibeon in which Abner was badly beaten. Joab did not push his victory home, though in the pursuit Asahel met his death at Abner's hand.

The power of Ishbosheth dwindled. He finally quarrelled with Abner, the mainstay of his throne, who at once opened negotiations with David. Michal, Saul's daughter, espoused to David and taken from him, was restored to him. Thereupon David accepted the terms of the Israelite chiefs sent by Abner, and was declared king of Israel. The murder of Abner by Joab, and of Ishbosheth by two of his captains, both of which acts David strongly disavowed, removed all possible opposition.

(3) The Philistines now declared war, alarmed partly by the consolidation of Judah and Israel into one kingdom, partly by David's brilliant capture of the fortress of Jerusalem. In two campaigns David freed Israel from Philistine oppression.

(4) One of his first acts was to make Jerusalem his capital. He fortified it; built a shrine for the Ark, which he restored to Israel; and raised a palace on Zion, with barracks for his body-guard.

He also turned his attention to Moab, Ammon, Edom and Syria. His wars were everywhere successful. He extended the northern border of Israel as far as the Euphrates ; established a sort of headship over the nations of Palestine ; strengthened himself with alliances; organised the government of the kingdom.

(5) The darkest stain upon David's fair name, his adultery with Bathsheba and the murder of Uriah, came about in connexion with the Ammonite war. From that time his life was troubled by domestic griefs. His eldest son Amnon committed a foul crime, for which he was killed by Absalom. Absalom fled, was forgiven, but treacherously stirred up a revolt against his father. David was forced to flee into Gilead. There the battle was fought, which resulted in the overthrow and death of Absalom. From the smouldering ashes of this rebellion, broke out another headed by Sheba, a member of Saul's tribe. This however was quickly quenched. Apparently tribal jealousy, especially between Judah and Benjamin, remained strong. Peace depended upon holding a precarious balance between the two.

(6) David had conceived a wish to build a temple for Jehovah, but was not permitted to carry it out. He made vast preparation for the building which Solomon was destined to complete (1 Chron. xxviii. f.). His death and Solomon's accession are recorded in 1 Kings i.

(7) David's reign was the Golden Age of Israel. It was the type of the kingdom of the Messiah, 'David's son.' Under his leadership, Israel, from a federation of tribes imperfectly united, and much oppressed by powerful neighbours, became a kingdom with vastly extended borders, 'the head or the nations' of Syria, renowned for power, wealth and civilization. This was brought about by the following means :

(a) David's military skill. Like other great leaders he also attracted to himself a circle of great soldiers.

(b) Much too was owing to his political sagacity. He knew when to be stern, and when to conciliate. Personal charm and tact helped to smooth over difficulties. He could wait for his opportunity, and at the right moment act with decision. He had also the wisdom to use the advice of shrewd counsellors.

(*c*) But the chief secret of Israel's success was the religious attitude of the king. Realising his position as theocratic king (see p. xiv.), he harmonised religious and secular authority. All the elements making for righteousness were in accord. King and prophet and priest worked together to make Jehovah's will the Law in Israel. Consequently religion advanced. Religious building is always an expression of religious feeling; and Solomon's gorgeous Temple was the result of the great revival of David's reign. When, on the other hand, David fell, it was the fall of a great religious leader, which often has disastrous consequences. These are drawn out with clear emphasis by the prophetic author of 2 Samuel. And yet David's religion is never more evident than in his penitence.

(8) *David's character.* We are fortunate in possessing a full and lifelike picture of David. We see him now tending sheep at Bethlehem, now prominent among the warriors of Saul's army; now a royal favourite, and now an outlaw; fleeing for his life with a band of outlaws, whose camp is the centre of religion and order; gradually winning his way from his desert stronghold to the throne of Israel; prophet, priest and poet as well as king; rough warrior and tactful politician; fierce conqueror, yet tender friend and father. And his character is as many-sided as his experience.

(*a*) He had a wonderful power of personal attraction. Jonathan, and at one time Saul, were his devoted friends. Even in adversity men (e.g. Ittai) clung to him.

(*b*) He was loved because he was loving. His Dirge is full of love. He was unselfish, generous and considerate. But he had the weakness of his qualities. He could not discipline his sons. He was tinged with Oriental sensualism, cruel when thwarted, resentful when wounded, touchy and impatient.

(*c*) He had the temperament of a soldier; he was personally brave; ready to risk his own life; fierce and ruthless in his anger. Yet even his least humane acts, such as the slaughter of the Moabites and Saul's seven sons, would not be thought cruel in that rude age.

(*d*) On the other hand, he was often an example of mercy and moderation. His followers thought him foolishly merciful. He readily forgave even those who had insulted and taken up arms against him (xix. 18 ff.).

(*e*) He was singularly trustful, because he was himself honest. His confidence in Abner and Amasa, and his lack of suspicion in the case of Absalom, seem almost quixotic. His dastardly trick against Uriah shews how far he had fallen from his true self.

To sum up, David's shortcomings were on the whole those of his race and times; but he was also 'the man after God's own heart,' and 'the darling of the songs of Israel,' a striking model of religious feeling and humanity to his contemporaries.

The characters of Joab and Absalom illustrate by contrast the greatness of David. Joab had great practical ability; he was faithful, upright, and even religious, as morality and religion were understood in those days. But he was entirely a man of his world; a typical Israelite, hard, narrow, unspiritual. Absalom had David's charm, but not his principle. He was David, without David's reverence for God and man.

IV. The Use of II Samuel.

(1) It contains *trustworthy history*. Most of the records preserved in it are extremely ancient ; they are not disfigured by legendary exaggerations and marvels. The *narrative* is simple, vivid and living, such as would be written by eyewitnesses. The *characters* are true to life ; there is no attempt to describe even David, Israel's hero though he was, as free from human sin and meanness. The *ideas and customs* of the time are faithfully represented.

(2) The chief *ethical value* of the book lies in its teaching by example. Each one of its characters carries its lesson. Joab's hardness repels us, but we admire his fidelity. Self-seeking greed is condemned in the Amalekite who brought the news of Saul's death ; hypocritical treachery in Ishbosheth's murderers ; cruel and undisciplined passion in Amnon ; devilish shrewdness in Jonadab, the son of Shimeah ; cold-blooded duplicity in Absalom. On the other hand how inspiring is the soldier-like simplicity of Uriah ; Nathan's fearlessness in rebuking an impenitent king ; devotion like that of Ittai, Hushai, and Barzillai ; the chivalrous daring of the three who broke through the Philistine lines to gratify David's longing for the water of Bethlehem ; Rizpah's faithful watch over her dead sons. The rich teaching of David's character has already been drawn out.

(3) The book is also the *record of a great crisis in the religious development of Israel* ; shewing how God taught His people, through David, higher ideas of Himself and His laws.

(*a*) David taught that Jehovah loved above all things justice and mercy. In those days men might be cruel, fierce, treacherous, unforgiving, and still religious. Joab in killing Abner, and Ishbosheth's murderers, thought they were carrying out God's wishes. David, on the other hand, felt that blood-revenge and murder were wrong, because God is merciful and just. He could take no pleasure in cruelty and treachery. The rich man in Nathan's parable was condemned 'because he had no pity.' David, in wronging Uriah, had wronged Jehovah still more ; he had 'despised the word of the Lord, to do that which was evil in His sight.' In contrast with the custom of his time, he set an example of mercifulness ; especially in his treatment of Abner, Saul's family, Absalom, Shimei, Amasa, and most of his foreign foes.

(*b*) With a deeper insight into the Divine Nature, came more spiritual views of His methods of revealing His will. The use of Urim and Thummim (ii. 1) seems to have died out. Three causes contributed to this : (1) The Ark was recovered. This was the most august symbol of Jehovah's Presence. Having it, men thought less of other symbols, such as the ephod that carried the lots. So in the Procession to Jerusalem (vi. 13), David sought to learn God's will by sacrificing before the Ark. (2) Again the living voice of inspired men, prophets and seers, assumed greater importance. Nathan and Gad are among the earliest of the great prophetic band, whose inspiration forms one of the grandest characteristics of Israel. (3) Another cause was the growth of David's own consciousness of his duty, as Jehovah's viceroy, of governing, as God governs, in righteousness and mercy. He learned to know Him from his own experience of Him.

(*c*) Out of this better knowledge of God sprang a new faith. David learned to trust himself to God's care. He no longer asked to know the future ; he even refused to allow the Ark to accompany him in his flight. His faith in the Divine Presence and Power no longer depended upon symbols (xv. 25 f.). Again, he prayed and fasted for his dying child ; but when God declared His will by taking the child, he bowed to that will and resumed his usual life (xii. 21 ff.). Such trust and submission were more than the courtiers could understand.

(*d*) Out of this period of religious revival arose much subsequent legislation. Laws grow out of precedents. Jehovah's disapproval of an act was marked by disaster. This manifestation formed a precedent. So laws guarding the inviolability of holy things might spring out of such events as the death of Uzzah (vi. 7 f.), a disaster quite unexpected. David's unhappy marriage with the princess of Geshur might lead to the prohibition of foreign marriages. The Court Record (ix.–xx.) is a vivid comment on the evils of polygamy. The accounts of the Famine (ch. xxi.) and the Plague (ch. xxiv.), events by which Jehovah manifested His anger at a breach of covenant with heathen, and His disapproval of the establishment of a standing army, are probably from a collection of such precedents.

(*e*) The record of David's reign is also prophetic, inasmuch as it points onward to the time of the Messiah. David being the typical theocratic king, ruling on earth as Jehovah's viceroy, was the fit recipient of the Messianic promise (vii. 12 ff.), that of his race should spring the Messiah, God's Son.

In the dark days, when nation and royal family sank into insignificance, this hope never died out of the heart of Israel.

V. The Difference between Samuel and Chronicles.

The Chronicler wrote about 300 B.C., long after the Exile, when the customs of David's days (1000 B.C.) had been altered and forgotten. He wished to tell the story of Israel before the Exile in such a way that his contemporaries might learn the importance of religious observances. He used the history as a text or illustration for a sermon. The Jews called such literature Midrash, that is, the free adaptation of national records for purposes of exhortation and edification. It was, no doubt, most useful in those terrible days when both the Jewish nation and its religion seemed in danger of being overwhelmed by the pressure of the great empires that laid heavy hands upon Palestine. We may notice two characteristics of Chronicles. (1) The story is made more vivid to the Jews of that time by being associated with *contemporary customs* ; just as mediaeval painters often drew the men of the Bible in Florentine or Venetian dress. (2) *The picture of David is considerably idealised.* The difficulties that kept him from the throne, his fall, and the troubles of his later years, are omitted.

ANALYSIS OF II SAMUEL.

A. *David, King of Judah,* i.–iv.

    Ch. i. Tidings of Saul's Death. David's Dirge.
        ii. David, King at Hebron ; Ishbosheth, King at Mahanaim. Battle of Gibeon.
       iii. Civil War. Abner's Overtures to David.
       iv. The Murder of Ishbosheth.

B. *David, King of Israel,* v.–viii.

    Ch. v. Capture of Jerusalem. Philistine Wars.
       vi. The Bringing of the Ark to Zion.
      vii. The Promise to David's House.
     viii. Summary of David's Wars and Government.

C. *The Court Record,* ix.–xx.

    Ch. ix. David and Mephibosheth.
       x. The Ammonite War.
      xi. David's Fall.
     xii. David's Repentance.
    xiii. Amnon's Crime and Death.
    xiv. The Recall of Absalom.
    xv.–xix. Absalom's Rebellion.
    xx. Sheba's Revolt.

D. *Appendix,* xxi.–xxiv.

    Ch. xxi. 1–14. The Famine.
    xxi. 15–22, xxiii. 8–39. David's Heroes.
    xxii. Song of Thanksgiving.
    xxiii. 1–7. David's Last Words.
    xxiv. The Plague.

THE

SECOND BOOK OF SAMUEL

A. David, King of Judah. I.–IV.

i. 1–16. *How David received the News of Saul's Death.*

AND it came to pass after the death of Saul, when
David was returned from the slaughter of the Amalekites,
and David had abode two days in Ziklag ; it came even 2
to pass on the third day, that, behold, a man came out of
the camp from Saul with his clothes rent, and earth upon
his head : and so it was, when he came to David, that he
fell to the earth, and did obeisance. And David said 3
unto him, From whence comest thou ? And he said
unto him, Out of the camp of Israel am I escaped. And 4
David said unto him, How went the matter ? I pray thee,
tell me. And he answered, The people are fled from the
battle, and many of the people also are fallen and dead ;
and Saul and Jonathan his son are dead also. And David 5

---

i. 1. And it came &c. Carrying on 1 Sam. xxxi. The
two books form only one in the Hebrew. A band of Arabs had
looted Keilah, David's headquarters, in his absence. After a
successful pursuit he was resting at Ziklag (somewhere in the
Negeb, or south country), where the news of Saul's death reached
him.

2. the third day. After David had reached Ziklag.

a man came. Runners were the usual news-carriers in
Palestine, horses being scarce (cf. Ahimaaz and the Cushite,
ch. xviii.). From Mt Gilboa, the scene of the battle, to Ziklag
was about 100 miles.

3. escaped. The one word tells the story of disaster.

4. Note David's anxiety to hear ; the man's hesitation to tell
(cf. a similar reticence xviii. 32). This and the battle of Aphek
(1 Sam. iv.) were two of the worst disasters in the annals of
Israel.

H.   1

said unto the young man that told him, How knowest
6 thou that Saul and Jonathan his son be dead? And the
young man that told him said, As I happened by chance
upon mount Gilboa, behold, Saul leaned upon his spear ;
and, lo, the chariots and the horsemen followed hard after
7 him. And when he looked behind him, he saw me, and
8 called unto me. And I answered, Here am I. And he
said unto me, Who art thou? And I answered him, I am
9 an Amalekite. And he said unto me, Stand, I pray thee,
beside me, and slay me, for anguish hath taken hold of
10 me; because my life is yet whole in me. So I stood
beside him, and slew him, because I was sure that he
could not live after that he was fallen : and I took the
crown that was upon his head, and the bracelet that was
on his arm, and have brought them hither unto my lord.
11 Then David took hold on his clothes, and rent them ; and
12 likewise all the men that were with him : and they
mourned, and wept, and fasted until even, for Saul, and
for Jonathan his son, and for the people of the LORD, and
for the house of Israel ; because they were fallen by the

---

6. As I happened. The Amalekite was either a slave or a
camp follower. His account of Saul's death does not agree with
that in 1 Sam. xxxi. There, Saul killed himself; and other de-
tails differ. This account (6–10, 13–16) may be taken from
some other document. In the confusion of defeat different ver-
sions would be published. (See Introd. p. ix.)

9. anguish (marg. 'giddiness'). If Saul became dizzy in his
flight and was seen leaning upon his sword for support, that
would explain how the report spread that he had fallen upon
his sword (1 Sam. xxxi. 4).

10. crown. A small circlet worn round the helmet.

bracelet. Such as are seen on the monuments of Assyrian and
Egyptian kings, and are still worn by Eastern monarchs.

12. until even. Easterns reckon the day from sunset to
sunset.

the people of the Lord. The fallen troops were Jehovah's
consecrated warriors fighting His battles against His foes, i.e.
foreigners, worshippers of foreign and rival gods (Introd.
p. xv.).

sword. And David said unto the young man that told 13
him, Whence art thou? And he answered, I am the son
of a stranger, an Amalekite. And David said unto him, 14
How wast thou not afraid to put forth thine hand to
destroy the LORD'S anointed? And David called one of 15
the young men, and said, Go near, and fall upon him.
And he smote him that he died. And David said unto 16
him, Thy blood be upon thy head; for thy mouth hath
testified against thee, saying, I have slain the LORD'S
anointed.

17-27.　*David's Dirge.*

This sublime song of David is one of the oldest passages in the
Old Testament. A later poet, writing in David's name, would
undoubtedly (1) have recalled in some way Saul's persecution,
and (2) have given a more distinctly religious tone to the poem.
It was at first handed down traditionally (hence the text is in
parts so corrupt that it is sometimes almost impossible to know the
exact meaning): then it found a place in the Book of Jashar,
whence the compiler of Samuel took it.

And David lamented with this lamentation over Saul 17
and over Jonathan his son: and he bade them teach the 18
children of Judah *the song of* the bow: behold, it is written
in the book of Jashar.

13.　a stranger (Heb. *gêr*). One living in Israel as a free
man, though of foreign race.

14. For David's own reverence for Saul's sacred person, see
1 Sam. xxiv. 6, xxvi. 11, 16. Saul's armour-bearer dared not
kill him even at his own request (*ib.* xxxi. 4).

17. It was usual among the ancients to chant dirges over
fallen heroes. So David sang over Abner (iii. 33 f.), and
Jeremiah over Josiah (2 Chron. xxxv. 25).

18.　the song of the bow. Not a likely title for the dirge.
Probably the text is corrupt. 'The song of' is not in the
Hebrew; and 'the bow' is not in the LXX. 'And he bade
them' means ' and he said '; which seems like the introduction
to the song. Transposing the clause to the end of the verse, and
omitting 'the song of the bow,' we can read, slightly changing
the text, 'And he said, Weep, O Judah.'

the book of Jashar. Probably a collection of ancient national
poetry, commemorating the great events and heroes of Hebrew
history (Josh. x. 13).

19 Thy glory, O Israel, is slain upon thy high places!
     How are the mighty fallen!
20 Tell it not in Gath,
       Publish it not in the streets of Ashkelon;
     Lest the daughters of the Philistines rejoice,
     Lest the daughters of the uncircumcised triumph.
21 Ye mountains of Gilboa,
       Let there be no dew nor rain upon you, neither fields
         of offerings:
     For there the shield of the mighty was vilely cast away,
     The shield of Saul, not anointed with oil.
22 From the blood of the slain, from the fat of the
       mighty,
     The bow of Jonathan turned not back,
     And the sword of Saul returned not empty.
23 Saul and Jonathan were lovely and pleasant in their
       lives,
     And in their death they were not divided;

---

19. The supreme disgrace was that the Philistines, who were lowlanders, should have routed so utterly the flower of Israel's chivalry among their native hills.

20. This verse is an excellent example of the parallelism, or repetition of the same idea in varying words, which is the chief characteristic of Hebrew poetry. Cf. *vv.* 22, 23.

21. **fields of offerings.** David curses the very ground that drank the blood of Israel's heroes. But the text appears to be corrupt. One early Greek version has, ' O mountains of death.'

vilely cast away. i.e. cast away and defiled with dust.

not anointed with oil. Either (1) of the shield, left uncared for: or (2) of Saul (marg. 'as of one not anointed'); as though it were the shield of a common mortal, not a king, its glory gone with the life of its mighty lord.

22. Saul's sword and Jonathan's bow were like tireless birds of prey.

23. **lovely and pleasant** (or 'kindly'). This throws light upon Saul's real character before it was darkened by disease; brave, heroic, generous, tender to his sons. David never ceased to love and revere him, even when persecuted by him. This generous consideration for the affliction of his enemy shews the nobility of his own nature.

They were swifter than eagles,
They were stronger than lions.
Ye daughters of Israel, weep over Saul,   24
Who clothed you in scarlet delicately,
Who put ornaments of gold upon your apparel.
How are the mighty fallen in the midst of the battle !   25
Jonathan is slain upon thy high places.
I am distressed for thee, my brother Jonathan :   26
Very pleasant hast thou been unto me:
Thy love to me was wonderful,
Passing the love of women.
How are the mighty fallen,   27
And the weapons of war perished !

ii. 1–4 a.   David, King of Judah.

And it came to pass after this, that David inquired of   2
the LORD, saying, Shall I go up into any of the cities of
Judah? And the LORD said unto him, Go up. And David
said, Whither shall I go up? And he said, Unto Hebron.
So David went up thither, and his two wives also, Ahinoam   2
the Jezreelitess, and Abigail the wife of Nabal the Carmelite. And his men that were with him did David bring   3

---

24. In his earlier years Saul had greatly bettered the position
of Israel by his military successes. Probably disease had robbed
him (as Napoleon) of his skill.

27. the weapons of war. i.e. Saul and Jonathan.

ii. 1. David inquired of the Lord. Patient reliance on the
Divine Will was one of David's chief virtues. The method of
inquiry seems to have been by the ephod, probably a portable
case or pouch holding the sacred lots (Urim and Thummim). A
question was asked and the lots were cast, one signifying 'yes'
and the other 'no.'

Go up. From low-lying Ziklag, where he had been under the
protection of the Philistines apparently in active hostility against
Judah (1 Sam. xxvii. 10–12).

Hebron. The chief town of Judah, strongly situated.

2. Jezreel and Carmel were small places near Hebron, not the
more famous places of the same name in Northern Israel.

For David's romantic wooing of Abigail at Carmel, see 1 Sam.
xxv.

up, every man with his household: and they dwelt in the
4 cities of Hebron. And the men of Judah came, and
there they anointed David king over the house of Judah.

4*b*–7. *David's Embassy to Gilead.*

And they told David, saying, The men of Jabesh-gilead
5 were they that buried Saul. And David sent messengers
unto the men of Jabesh-gilead, and said unto them,
Blessed be ye of the LORD, that ye have shewed this
kindness unto your lord, even unto Saul, and have buried
6 him. And now the LORD shew kindness and truth unto
you: and I also will requite you this kindness, because
7 ye have done this thing. Now therefore let your hands
be strong, and be ye valiant: for Saul your lord is dead,
and also the house of Judah have anointed me king over
them.

8–11. *Ishbosheth, King of Israel.*

8   Now Abner the son of Ner, captain of Saul's host, had
taken Ish-bosheth the son of Saul, and brought him over

---

4. they anointed David king. The pouring of oil over the
king's head endowed him with the Spirit of Jehovah and
made his person sacred. David was acceptable to the men
of Judah, both as a clansman, and as one who had given them
substantial proofs of his friendship (see 1 Sam. xxx. 26 ff.).

5. this kindness. Saul had earned the devotion of the
Gileadites by his succour of Jabesh from the Ammonites (1 Sam.
xi.).

7. let your hands be strong. Being king *de facto*, and
possibly ignorant of Ishbosheth's claim, David urges Gilead to
prepare for war against the Philistines. Eastern Israel, however,
held to Saul's house, though the kingship was not yet hereditary.

8. Abner. Saul's first cousin (1 Sam. xiv. 50) and commander-in-chief, and now the chief support of Saul's house. To
have held together Northern and Eastern Israel for seven years
in the face of Judaean, Philistine and probably Moabite and
Ammonite hostility, proves him a man of skill and power.
David regarded him with great respect (iii. 38 ; 1 Sam. xxvi. 15).

Ishbosheth. His name was Ishbaal (1 Chron. viii. 33) = man
of Baal'; but the editor, to avoid using the word Baal, altered

to Mahanaim; and he made him king over Gilead, and 9
over the Ashurites, and over Jezreel, and over Ephraim,
and over Benjamin, and over all Israel. (Ish-bosheth 10
Saul's son was forty years old when he began to reign
over Israel, and he reigned two years.) But the house of
Judah followed David. And the time that David was 11
king in Hebron over the house of Judah was seven years
and six months.

12-17. *Abner's Expedition against Gibeon.*

And Abner the son of Ner, and the servants of Ish- 12
bosheth the son of Saul, went out from Mahanaim to
Gibeon. And Joab the son of Zeruiah, and the servants 13
of David, went out, and met them by the pool of Gibeon;
and they sat down, the one on the one side of the pool,
and the other on the other side of the pool. And Abner 14
said to Joab, Let the young men, I pray thee, arise and

---

the name to Ishbosheth ('man of shame'). So Mephibosheth
(iv. 4) stands for Meribbaal (1 Chron. viii. 34), Jerubbesheth
(xi. 21) for Jerubbaal (Judg. vii. 1).

Mahanaim. An important town E. of the Jordan, N. of the
Jabbok. It was afterwards David's headquarters during Absalom's rebellion (xvii. 24).

9. Gilead. All Israelite territory, E. of the Jordan.

the Ashurites &c. All the rest of Israel except Judah.

10. two years. David was king in Hebron 7½ years. Ish-
bosheth must have reigned in Mahanaim for a similar period.
Perhaps 5½ years were occupied in establishing his position: and
for two years only was his rule acknowledged.

12. It is possible that Abner had heard that the Gibeonites,
who had a blood-feud with Saul (xxi. 1 ff.), were helping David.

13. Joab. The first mention of this striking personality.
He was David's nephew, son of Zeruiah, David's sister. He
was a skilful and successful commander-in-chief. He defeated
the Ammonites, capturing their capital; conquered Edom;
crushed the rebellions of Absalom and Sheba. He killed by
treachery his two possible rivals, Abner and Amasa. He was
fierce and revengeful, and, though entirely faithful to David, he
had no sympathy with his religious aspirations and reforms.

14. To avoid civil war Abner proposed that the question
should be decided by a combat of picked champions.

15 play before us. And Joab said, Let them arise. Then
they arose and went over by number; twelve for Benjamin,
and for Ish-bosheth the son of Saul, and twelve of the
16 servants of David. And they caught every one his fellow
by the head, and *thrust* his sword in his fellow's side ; so
they fell down together : wherefore that place was called
17 Helkath-hazzurim, which is in Gibeon. And the battle
was very sore that day ; and Abner was beaten, and the
men of Israel, before the servants of David.

18-23. *The Death of Asahel.*

18 And the three sons of Zeruiah were there, Joab, and
Abishai, and Asahel : and Asahel was as light of foot as
19 a wild roe. And Asahel pursued after Abner; and in
going he turned not to the right hand nor to the left from
20 following Abner. Then Abner looked behind him, and
21 said, Is it thou, Asahel? And he answered, It is I. And
Abner said to him, Turn thee aside to thy right hand or
to thy left, and lay thee hold on one of the young men,
and take thee his armour. But Asahel would not turn
22 aside from following of him. And Abner said again to
Asahel, Turn thee aside from following me : wherefore
should I smite thee to the ground? how then should I
23 hold up my face to Joab thy brother? Howbeit he
refused to turn aside: wherefore Abner with the hinder
end of the spear smote him in the belly, that the spear
came out behind him ; and he fell down there, and died in
the same place: and it came to pass, that as many as came
to the place where Asahel fell down and died stood still.

---

16. Helkath-hazzurim. 'The field of sharp knives'
(marg.). The LXX reads Helkath-hazzodim, 'the field of
liers in wait.'

21. Turn thee aside. If Asahel desires spoil, let him attack
some less expert warrior. Asahel, the youngest of the three
brothers, was probably still a youth.

23. the hinder end of the spear. Being tipped with iron, a
strong stroke backward was sufficient to kill.

24-32. *The Pursuit.*

But Joab and Abishai pursued after Abner: and the sun 24
went down when they were come to the hill of Ammah,
that lieth before Giah by the way of the wilderness of
Gibeon. And the children of Benjamin gathered them- 25
selves together after Abner, and became one band, and
stood on the top of an hill. Then Abner called to Joab, 26
and said, Shall the sword devour for ever? knowest thou
not that it will be bitterness in the latter end? how long
shall it be then, ere thou bid the people return from
following their brethren? And Joab said, As God liveth, 27
if thou hadst not spoken, surely then in the morning the
people had gone away, nor followed every one his brother.
So Joab blew the trumpet, and all the people stood still, 28
and pursued after Israel no more, neither fought they any
more. And Abner and his men went all that night 29
through the Arabah; and they passed over Jordan, and
went through all Bithron, and came to Mahanaim. And 30
Joab returned from following Abner: and when he had
gathered all the people together, there lacked of David's
servants nineteen men and Asahel. But the servants of 31
David had smitten of Benjamin, and of Abner's men,
so that three hundred and threescore men died. And 32
they took up Asahel, and buried him in the sepulchre of
his father, which was in Beth-lehem. And Joab and his

---

24. the hill of Ammah &c. These obscure landmarks were
evidently familiar to the writer.

25. Abner rallies his men for a last stand.

26 f. Abner appeals to Joab not to embitter further the
hostility between Israel and Judah by fresh bloodshed. Joab
throws the responsibility of fighting upon Abner's challenge
(*v.* 14). The armies had not come to fight.

29. the Arabah. The Jordan Valley. This Abner's men
crossed, and mounted by the **Bithron** ('ravine'), a watercourse
leading them eastward to Mahanaim.

30 f. The disparity between Joab's and Abner's losses shews
that the Israelite levies were no match for David's veterans.

men went all night, and the day brake upon them at
Hebron.

iii. 1-5. *David strengthens his Position.*

3 Now there was long war between the house of Saul
and the house of David: and David waxed stronger and
stronger, but the house of Saul waxed weaker and
weaker.

2 And unto David were sons born in Hebron: and his
3 firstborn was Amnon, of Ahinoam the Jezreelitess; and
his second, Chileab, of Abigail the wife of Nabal the
Carmelite; and the third, Absalom the son of Maacah
4 the daughter of Talmai king of Geshur; and the fourth,
Adonijah the son of Haggith; and the fifth, Shephatiah
5 the son of Abital; and the sixth, Ithream, of Eglah David's
wife.   These were born to David in Hebron.

6-11. *Abner's Disaffection.*

6 And it came to pass, while there was war between the
house of Saul and the house of David, that Abner made
7 himself strong in the house of Saul.   Now Saul had a
concubine, whose name was Rizpah, the daughter of

---

iii. 1. long war. Probably no more than petty raids. David's
policy was to conciliate, not coerce, the followers of Ishbosheth.
He was also too far-seeing and patriotic to weaken Israel by unnecessary civil war in the face of the Philistine oppression.

2. Kings multiplied wives in order to strengthen their
dynasty. The evil effects of polygamy are amply illustrated in
the family history of David. (Introd. p. xxii.) Of these six
sons Amnon, Absalom and Adonijah figure unfavourably in the
succeeding history.

3. Geshur. A small Syrian kingdom lying on the N.E.
border of Israel (xv. 8). Marriage with foreign women was forbidden at a later time in Ex. xxxiv. 16, Deut. vii. 3: but this
prohibition cannot have been known to David. This marriage
with the Syrian princess bore luckless fruit in the unhappy Tamar
and the infamous Absalom.

6. made himself strong in &c. There was no one to check
Abner's overbearing masterfulness.

7. Rizpah (see xxi. 8 ff.). In marrying her, who had be-

Aiah: and *Ish-bosheth* said to Abner, Wherefore hast thou gone in unto my father's concubine? Then was 8 Abner very wroth for the words of Ish-bosheth, and said, Am I a dog's head that belongeth to Judah? This day do I shew kindness unto the house of Saul thy father, to his brethren, and to his friends, and have not delivered thee into the hand of David, and yet thou chargest me this day with a fault concerning this woman. God do so 9 to Abner, and more also, if, as the LORD hath sworn to David, I do not even so to him; to translate the kingdom 10 from the house of Saul, and to set up the throne of David over Israel and over Judah, from Dan even to Beer-sheba. And he could not answer Abner another word, because he 11 feared him.

12-16. *Negotiations.*

And Abner sent messengers to David on his behalf, 12 saying, Whose is the land? saying *also*, Make thy league with me, and, behold, my hand shall be with thee, to bring about all Israel unto thee. And he said, Well; 13 I will make a league with thee: but one thing I require of thee, that is, thou shalt not see my face, except thou

---

longed to the harem of the late king, Abner was, according to the ideas of the time, assuming royal state. Cf. xii. 8.

8. Am I a dog's head? In Eastern towns dogs roam half wild in the streets, living upon refuse. Abner complains that a man of his importance, and the mainstay of Saul's house, should be insulted by such a rebuke and suspicion.

9. as the Lord hath sworn to David. No such Divine oath is recorded : yet there seems to have been a feeling that David's succession to Saul was according to God's Will. The religious sense of Israel was for David, and against Ishbosheth.

10. from Dan &c. As we say 'From John o' Groat's to Land's End' : from extreme north to extreme south.

11. Ishbosheth was a mere puppet-king in Abner's hands.

12. on his behalf. Abner opens negotiations in the name of Ishbosheth.

Whose is the land ? While there are two claimants it belongs to neither. If David and Abner could agree, it would be David's.

first bring Michal Saul's daughter, when thou comest to
14 see my face.   And David sent messengers to Ish-bosheth
Saul's son, saying, Deliver me my wife Michal, whom I
betrothed to me for an hundred foreskins of the Philistines.
15 And Ish-bosheth sent, and took her from her husband,
16 even from Paltiel the son of Laish.   And her husband
went with her, weeping as he went, and followed her to
Bahurim.   Then said Abner unto him, Go, return: and
he returned.

17–21.   *The Treaty.*

17   And Abner had communication with the elders of
Israel, saying, In times past ye sought for David to be
18 king over you: now then do it: for the LORD hath spoken
of David, saying, By the hand of my servant David I
will save my people Israel out of the hand of the Philistines,
19 and out of the hand of all their enemies.   And Abner also
spake in the ears of Benjamin: and Abner went also to
speak in the ears of David in Hebron all that seemed
20 good to Israel, and to the whole house of Benjamin.   So
Abner came to David to Hebron, and twenty men with
him.   And David made Abner and the men that were
21 with him a feast.   And Abner said unto David, I will
arise and go, and will gather all Israel unto my lord the
king, that they may make a covenant with thee, and that
thou mayest reign over all that thy soul desireth.   And
David sent Abner away; and he went in peace.

---

13.   Michal.   David demands public reparation for the wrong
Saul had done him ; he also seeks to strengthen his position as
Saul's son-in-law.

17.   ye sought for David &c.   One of the sources of Ish-
bosheth's weakness had been the existence of a David-party
among the Israelite chiefs.

19.   Benjamin.   Saul's tribe would need special inducement
to consent to the election of a Judaean.   Some, e.g. Shimei and
Sheba, seem never to have laid aside their opposition.   The
chiefs sent their terms by Abner, and David accepted them.

22–27. *The Murder of Abner.*

And, behold, the servants of David and Joab came from a 22
foray, and brought in a great spoil with them: but Abner
was not with David in Hebron; for he had sent him away,
and he was gone in peace.   When Joab and all the host 23
that was with him were come, they told Joab, saying,
Abner the son of Ner came to the king, and he hath sent
him away, and he is gone in peace.   Then Joab came to 24
the king, and said, What hast thou done? behold, Abner
came unto thee; why is it that thou hast sent him away,
and he is quite gone?   Thou knowest Abner the son of 25
Ner, that he came to deceive thee, and to know thy going
out and thy coming in, and to know all that thou doest.
And when Joab was come out from David, he sent 26
messengers after Abner, and they brought him back from
the well of Sirah: but David knew it not.   And when 27
Abner was returned to Hebron, Joab took him aside into
the midst of the gate to speak with him quietly, and smote
him there in the belly, that he died, for the blood of Asahel
his brother.

28–30. *David's Curse on Joab.*

And afterward when David heard it, he said, I and my 28
kingdom are guiltless before the LORD for ever from the

---

22. a foray. David's revenue was still largely raised by
plundering expeditions against the hostile tribes of the southern
desert.

24. Then Joab came &c. Joab, cunning and cruel himself,
could neither give a foe credit for good faith nor understand
David's trustful tenderness to his Hebrew enemies.   His brusque
speech to the king illustrates the independent spirit of the Hebrew
sheikhs.

27. According to the law of blood-revenge both Joab and
David were bound to take Abner's life.   David however had
risen to the higher conception of the law of mercy.   No doubt
Joab was fully aware that there was not room for two such
masterful wills as his own and Abner's in one army.

28. I and my kingdom are guiltless. By disavowing all

29 blood of Abner the son of Ner: let it fall upon the head
   of Joab, and upon all his father's house; and let there
   not fail from the house of Joab one that hath an issue, or
   that is a leper, or that leaneth on a staff, or that falleth by
30 the sword, or that lacketh bread. So Joab and Abishai
   his brother slew Abner, because he had killed their brother
   Asahel at Gibeon in the battle.

31-39.   *The Burial of Abner.*

31   And David said to Joab, and to all the people that were
   with him, Rend your clothes, and gird you with sackcloth,
   and mourn before Abner. And king David followed the
32 bier. And they buried Abner in Hebron: and the king
   lifted up his voice, and wept at the grave of Abner; and
33 all the people wept. And the king lamented for Abner,
   and said,

   Should Abner die as a fool dieth?

34   Thy hands were not bound, nor thy feet put into
      fetters:
      As a man falleth before the children of iniquity, so
      didst thou fall.

35 And all the people wept again over him. And all the
   people came to cause David to eat bread while it was
   yet day; but David sware, saying, God do so to me, and
   more also, if I taste bread, or aught else, till the sun be
36 down. And all the people took notice of it, and it pleased
   them: as whatsoever the king did pleased all the people.

---

responsibility for the murder, David removed the dangerous
suspicions of Abner's party.

29. one that hath an issue, or that is a leper. These two
diseases rendered the sufferer ceremonially unclean and exiled
him from worship.

30. Abishai. It is not said what part he took in the murder,
but he would naturally associate himself with Joab.

33 f. Should Abner die &c. A pitiful death for a hero!
Like a bound criminal, he could not stir a limb to save himself.
But it was treachery, not crime, that made him defenceless.

So all the people and all Israel understood that day that 37
it was not of the king to slay Abner the son of Ner. And 38
the king said unto his servants, Know ye not that there is
a prince and a great man fallen this day in Israel? And 39
I am this day weak, though anointed king; and these men
the sons of Zeruiah be too hard for me: the LORD reward
the wicked doer according to his wickedness.

iv. 1-7. *The Murder of Ishbosheth.*

And when *Ish-bosheth*, Saul's son, heard that Abner was **4**
dead in Hebron, his hands became feeble, and all the
Israelites were troubled. And *Ish-bosheth*, Saul's son, 2
had two men that were captains of bands: the name of
the one was Baanah, and the name of the other Rechab,
the sons of Rimmon the Beerothite, of the children of
Benjamin: (for Beeroth also is reckoned to Benjamin:
and the Beerothites fled to Gittaim, and have been 3
sojourners there until this day.)

Now Jonathan, Saul's son, had a son that was lame of 4
his feet. He was five years old when the tidings came of
Saul and Jonathan out of Jezreel, and his nurse took him

---

39. I am this day weak. Not from youth and inexperience,
but because even a king cannot go against the customs of his
race, though he knows them to be wrong. The sons of Zeruiah
were hard, but blood-revenge was the law. David could only
leave it to Jehovah to vindicate His higher laws. The popularity
of the king's action (*v.* 36) shews however that public opinion was
ripe for an advance. Under the strong central government of
the kings the law of blood-revenge died out. This entire account
shews the hostile attitude of a more enlightened age towards this
relic of heathen barbarism.

iv. 2. captains of bands. Their business was to supply the
royal revenue by plunder. Cf. iii. 22.

Beeroth. One of the Gibeonite cities in the Benjamite territory.
If these men were Beerothites (Gibeonites), and not true Benjamites, their action was probably one of vengeance, and connected with the feud between Saul and the Gibeonites (see ii. 12,
xxi. 1 ff.).

3. sojourners. Heb. *gêrim.* See i. 13.

up, and fled: and it came to pass, as she made haste to
flee, that he fell, and became lame. And his name was
Mephibosheth.

5 And the sons of Rimmon the Beerothite, Rechab and
Baanah, went, and came about the heat of the day to the
6 house of Ish-bosheth, as he took his rest at noon. And
they came thither into the midst of the house, as though
they would have fetched wheat; and they smote him in
the belly: and Rechab and Baanah his brother escaped.
7 Now when they came into the house, as he lay on his bed
in his bedchamber, they smote him, and slew him, and
beheaded him, and took his head, and went by the way of
the Arabah all night.

8–12. *The Reward of the Assassins.*

8 And they brought the head of Ish-bosheth unto David to
Hebron, and said to the king, Behold the head of Ish-
bosheth the son of Saul thine enemy, which sought thy
life; and the LORD hath avenged my lord the king this
9 day of Saul, and of his seed. And David answered
Rechab and Baanah his brother, the sons of Rimmon the
Beerothite, and said unto them, As the LORD liveth, who
10 hath redeemed my soul out of all adversity, when one
told me, saying, Behold, Saul is dead, thinking to have

---

4. Mephibosheth. His real name was Meribbaal ('the Lord
contends'). See ii. 8.

6, 7. Read with LXX, as in marg., 'And behold, the woman
that kept the door of the house was winnowing wheat, and she
slumbered and slept: and the brethren, Rechab and Baanah,
went privily into the house.' Ishbosheth was apparently deserted
by all but one female slave.

the Arabah. The Jordan Valley. It was 80 or 90 miles from
Mahanaim to Hebron.

8. the Lord &c. This seems to us horrible hypocrisy; but
the heathen idea that God cared less about morality than for
getting His plans carried out still lingered on.

9. As the Lord &c. David's reply shews the truer idea of
God, as One who delights in kindness and honesty.

10. when one told me. The writer of this account knows

brought good tidings, I took hold of him, and slew him in
Ziklag, which was the reward I gave him for his tidings.
How much more, when wicked men have slain a righteous 11
person in his own house upon his bed, shall I not now
require his blood of your hand, and take you away from
the earth? And David commanded his young men, and 12
they slew them, and cut off their hands and their feet, and
hanged them up beside the pool in Hebron. But they
took the head of Ish-bosheth, and buried it in the grave
of Abner in Hebron.

B. David, King of Israel. V.–VIII.

v. 1–5. *David made King of Israel.*

Then came all the tribes of Israel to David unto 5
Hebron, and spake, saying, Behold, we are thy bone
and thy flesh. In times past, when Saul was king over 2
us, it was thou that leddest out and broughtest in Israel:

---

nothing of the Amalekite who professed to have slain Saul
(i. 6 ff.). Perhaps that story was worked into the original
account to soften down the severity of David's action in killing
the bringer of the news merely for thinking that such news would
be a matter of rejoicing. But the older account, if it reveals
a fierceness terrible to a more civilised age, shews also a wonder-
fully unselfish magnanimity to a foe.

11. a righteous person. Another generous tribute to an
enemy.

take you away from the earth. Rather, 'put you away out
of the land.' Cf. Numb. xxxv. 33 f. Jehovah's land was defiled
by the blood of Jehovah's people; it can only be cleansed by the
blood of him that shed it. See also Gen. iv. 10.

12. their hands and their feet. The hands which had done
the deed and the feet which had carried them to their crime were
exposed before Jehovah at the pool, in expiation. David's
policy was to put down individual violence, and bring the
relations of man and man within the reign of law.

v. 1. the tribes of Israel. The northern tribes are meant.
They are led to elect David king on three grounds : (*a*) common
blood. (*b*) David's old military prowess as Saul's commander-in-
chief. Saul's jealousy shews that it was considerable. (*c*) God's
selection (note on iii. 9).

H.   **2**

and the LORD said to thee, Thou shalt feed my people
3 Israel, and thou shalt be prince over Israel. So all the
elders of Israel came to the king to Hebron; and king
David made a covenant with them in Hebron before the
LORD: and they anointed David king over Israel.

4   David was thirty years old when he began to reign, and
5 he reigned forty years. In Hebron he reigned over Judah
seven years and six months: and in Jerusalem he reigned
thirty and three years over all Israel and Judah.

6–8. *The Taking of Jerusalem.*

6 And the king and his men went to Jerusalem against the
Jebusites, the inhabitants of the land: which spake unto
David, saying, Except thou take away the blind and the
lame, thou shalt not come in hither: thinking, David
7 cannot come in hither. Nevertheless David took the
8 strong hold of Zion; the same is the city of David. And
David said on that day, Whosoever smiteth the Jebusites,

---

2. Thou shalt feed. As a shepherd. Cf. Ps. lxxviii. 70.

3. a covenant. This evidently meant preparation for war, as
the Philistines soon realised.

before the Lord. The king was Jehovah's viceroy.

4. thirty years old. The prime of life, when men began
their lifework in earnest. So Joseph (Gen. xli. 46) and our
Lord (Lc. iii. 23). Cf. Numb. iv. 3.

6. the Jebusites. A Canaanite tribe, called from their town
Jebus. They had never been conquered yet. David saw in
this fortress a capital that would be a centre of unity to the
loosely connected tribes which formed his kingdom. Hebron
was too far south. Jebus being moreover on the border of Judah
and Benjamin, the bitter jealousy between the two royal tribes
might be pacified by its choice. It was also easily accessible and
almost impregnable.

Except thou take away. The marg., 'Thou shalt not come
in hither, but the blind and the lame shall turn thee away,' gives
better sense. The Jebusites thought their fortress impregnable.

7. Jerusalem stands on two spurs running S. from the central
plateau of Palestine. Zion, David's city, was upon the eastern
spur.

let him get up to the watercourse, and *smite* the lame and
the blind, that are hated of David's soul. Wherefore
they say, There are the blind and the lame; he cannot
come into the house.

9–12. *The Court at Jerusalem.*

And David dwelt in the strong hold, and called it the city 9
of David. And David built round about from Millo and
inward. And David waxed greater and greater; for the 10
LORD, the God of hosts, was with him.

And Hiram king of Tyre sent messengers to David, 11
and cedar trees, and carpenters, and masons: and they
built David an house. And David perceived that the 12
LORD had established him king over Israel, and that he
had exalted his kingdom for his people Israel's sake.

13–16. *List of Sons born in Jerusalem.*

And David took him more concubines and wives out of 13
Jerusalem, after he was come from Hebron: and there

---

8. the watercourse. Some channel by which the water of
the fountain of Gibeon in the Valley of the Kidron was brought
up to the fortress. The text here is very obscure and probably
corrupt.

There are the blind &c. Probably a proverb, meaning (as
marg., 'The blind and the lame shall not come into the house')
that blind and lame are excluded from the Temple.

The Chronicler says that David offered the chief command to
him who first scaled the wall, and that Joab won the prize.

9. And David dwelt &c. He built a palace, a shrine,
barracks for his guards, and new and stronger fortifications.
This was a great advance upon Saul's simple court at Gibeah.

Millo. Rather, 'the Millo.' From a root = 'to fill.' Some
isolated prominent feature in the ramparts.

11. Hiram king of Tyre. Tyre, a commercial state, largely
dependent upon Israel for corn, would welcome the settled
government of David after the long period of disorder. Tyre
and Israel were usually allies (1 Kings v. 1 ff., xvi. 31).

13. And David took &c. Cf. iii. 2 n. David conciliated
the Jebusites by marriage, and by leaving them undisturbed in
their homes. See, e.g., the case of Araunah (xxiv. 16).

14 were yet sons and daughters born to David.   And these
   be the names of those that were born unto him in Jerusalem; Shammua, and Shobab, and Nathan, and Solomon,
15
16 and Ibhar, and Elishua; and Nepheg, and Japhia; and
   Elishama, and Eliada, and Eliphelet.

17–21.   *The First Philistine Campaign.*

David in Judah had been on friendly terms with the Philistines,
probably acknowledging himself their vassal.   His election as
king of Israel implied a determined effort to throw off the Philistine yoke.   By a brilliant and rapid stroke, he captured Jerusalem.
Perhaps the Jebusites had been subject to the Philistines.   The
latter lost no time in moving up to attack.   David, perhaps
leaving a garrison in Jerusalem, retired into a strong position,
probably Adullam (see xxiii. 13), where he lay hid.   Following
Divine direction he attacked them at Baal-perazim, and inflicted a
severe defeat upon them.   In their flight they left behind even
their sacred images.   These, the Chronicler states (1 Chr. xiv. 12),
David burnt in obedience to Deut. vii. 5, 25.   In this victory
the disgrace of the loss of the Ark at Aphek (1 Sam. iv. 11) was
wiped out.

17   And when the Philistines heard that they had anointed
     David king over Israel, all the Philistines went up to
     seek David; and David heard of it, and went down to
18 the hold.   Now the Philistines had come and spread
19 themselves in the valley of Rephaim.   And David in-
     quired of the LORD, saying, Shall I go up against the
     Philistines? wilt thou deliver them into mine hand? And
     the LORD said unto David, Go up: for I will certainly
20 deliver the Philistines into thine hand.   And David came
     to Baal-perazim, and David smote them there; and he
     said, The LORD hath broken mine enemies before me,
     like the breach of waters.   Therefore he called the name
21 of that place Baal-perazim.   And they left their images
     there, and David and his men took them away.

---

20.   In later times the name Baal was used only for the
Phoenician and Canaanite deities and was therefore avoided (see
ii. 8 note).   But at this early date David, in calling the place
Baal-perazim, used it as one of the titles of Jehovah.

22–25. *The Second Campaign.*

With a fresh force the Philistines came up again, probably intending to retake Jerusalem. Again they encamped S. of Jerusalem, in the Valley of Rephaim. This time David was directed to steal round to the rear of their position, near a wood of mulberry trees (or better, with marg., 'balsam trees'), and there wait until he heard the leaves pattering in the rising breeze, the first sign of a coming storm. When the storm burst in their faces, David charged; and again crushed them, driving them in headlong rout. In these two campaigns, which may have been prolonged, David threw off the Philistine yoke. He probably assumed the offensive and 'took the bridle of the mother-city out of the hands of the Philistines' (see note on viii. 1).

And the Philistines came up yet again, and spread ₂₂ themselves in the valley of Rephaim. And when David ₂₃ inquired of the LORD, he said, Thou shalt not go up: make a circuit behind them, and come upon them over against the mulberry trees. And it shall be, when thou ₂₄ hearest the sound of marching in the tops of the mulberry trees, that then thou shalt bestir thyself: for then is the LORD gone out before thee to smite the host of the Philistines. And David did so, as the LORD commanded ₂₅ him; and smote the Philistines from Geba until thou come to Gezer.

vi. 1–5. *How the Ark was brought from Kirjath-jearim.*

And David again gathered together all the chosen **6** men of Israel, thirty thousand. And David arose, and ₂ went with all the people that were with him, from Baale Judah, to bring up from thence the ark of God, which is called by the Name, even the name of the LORD of hosts

---

vi. 1. again. A third campaign, offensive on David's part. This great army could only be for military operations.

2. Baale Judah or Baalah (see 1 Chr. xiii. 6), i.e. Kirjath-jearim, the home of the Ark since its restoration by the Philistines.

the ark of God. An oblong wooden box, small enough to be carried on the shoulders of two men. As the symbol of Jehovah's Presence and their national unity, it was Israel's most treasured possession.

3 that sitteth upon the cherubim. And they set the ark
of God upon a new cart, and brought it out of the house
of Abinadab that was in the hill: and Uzzah and Ahio,
4 the sons of Abinadab, drave the new cart. And they
brought it out of the house of Abinadab, which was in
the hill, with the ark of God : and Ahio went before the
5 ark. And David and all the house of Israel played before
the LORD with all manner of *instruments made of* fir
wood, and with harps, and with psalteries, and with
timbrels, and with castanets, and with cymbals.

6–11.   *The Death of Uzzah.*

6 And when they came to the threshing-floor of Nacon,
Uzzah put forth *his hand* to the ark of God, and took
7 hold of it ; for the oxen stumbled. And the anger of the
LORD was kindled against Uzzah ; and God smote him
there for his error ; and there he died by the ark of God.
8 And David was displeased, because the LORD had broken
forth upon Uzzah : and he called that place Perez-uzzah,
9 unto this day. And David was afraid of the LORD that
day; and he said, How shall the ark of the LORD come
10 unto me? So David would not remove the ark of the
LORD unto him into the city of David ; but David carried
11 it aside into the house of Obed-edom the Gittite.   And

---

that sitteth upon the cherubim. The picture is of Jehovah
carried through the sky on the whirling thunder-cloud (cf. xxii. 11),
scattering His foes as He did in Rephaim (v. 24).

4.   And they brought...in the hill. This appears to have
been accidentally repeated by a copyist fron v. 3.

5.   harps and psalteries. Stringed instruments.

timbrels. Small drums struck by hand (like tambourines).

castanets, marg. 'sistra.' Probably instruments fitted with
metal rings, giving a tinkling sound when rattled.

7.   According to ancient ideas no holy object might be used in
an ordinary way, or touched by any but consecrated persons
without danger. The Ark was of course specially sacred.
Through this idea God taught His people His awful Majesty
and the need of reverence in approaching Him.

10.   Obed-edom. A native of Gath, so a sojourner (Heb. *gēr,*
see i. 13), who had settled in Israel and was allowed, among
other privileges, to take part in the national worship.

the ark of the LORD remained in the house of Obed-edom
the Gittite three months: and the LORD blessed Obed-
edom, and all his house.

12–19.　*How the Ark came to Jerusalem.*

And it was told king David, saying, The LORD hath 12
blessed the house of Obed-edom, and all that pertaineth
unto him, because of the ark of God. And David went
and brought up the ark of God from the house of Obed-
edom into the city of David with joy. And it was so, 13
that when they that bare the ark of the LORD had gone
six paces, he sacrificed an ox and a fatling. And David 14
danced before the LORD with all his might; and David
was girded with a linen ephod. So David and all the 15
house of Israel brought up the ark of the LORD with
shouting, and with the sound of the trumpet. And it 16
was so, as the ark of the LORD came into the city of
David, that Michal the daughter of Saul looked out at
the window, and saw king David leaping and dancing
before the LORD; and she despised him in her heart.
And they brought in the ark of the LORD, and set it in 17
its place, in the midst of the tent that David had pitched
for it: and David offered burnt offerings and peace

12.　The Lord hath blessed &c. Jehovah made it clear that His
Presence brought blessing, not destruction, upon those who
feared Him. Hence the 'joy.'

13.　they that bare the ark. It was carried, not driven;
and a solemn sacrifice was offered at starting.

A comparison of this account with that in 1 Chron. xv. is in-
structive as shewing the difference between the two books.

14.　And David danced. He whirled, like a dervish, before
the Ark. He was dressed, not in his flowing regal robes, but in
some slight linen dress, perhaps a loin-cloth.

16.　she despised him. The whirling prophets were not much
respected. When Saul joined them (a fact that Saul's daughter
perhaps did not know) his behaviour caused surprise. See
1 Sam. x. 10 f., xix. 23 f.

17.　David offered. He acted as priest as well as prophet and
king.

18 offerings before the LORD. And when David had made
an end of offering the burnt offering and the peace
offerings, he blessed the people in the name of the LORD
19 of hosts. And he dealt among all the people, even
among the whole multitude of Israel, both to men and
women, to every one a cake of bread, and a portion *of
flesh*, and a cake of raisins. So all the people departed
every one to his house.

20–23. *The Rebuke of Michal.*

20 Then David returned to bless his household. And Michal
the daughter of Saul came out to meet David, and said,
How glorious was the king of Israel to-day, who un-
covered himself to-day in the eyes of the handmaids of
his servants, as one of the vain fellows shamelessly
21 uncovereth himself! And David said unto Michal, *It
was* before the LORD, which chose me above thy father,
and above all his house, to appoint me prince over the
people of the LORD, over Israel : therefore will I play
22 before the LORD. And I will be yet more vile than thus,
and will be base in mine own sight : but of the handmaids
which thou hast spoken of, of them shall I be had in
23 honour. And Michal the daughter of Saul had no child
unto the day of her death.

vii. 1–3. *David's Design to build a Temple.*

7   And it came to pass, when the king dwelt in his house,
and the LORD had given him rest from all his enemies

---

21. It was before the Lord. Michal had accused him of
lowering his dignity by dancing as a dervish. He answers that
to humble himself in God's Presence could not degrade him either
in his own respect or his servants'.

vii. 1. the Lord had given him rest. This was not for many
years after his settling at Jerusalem. In point of time the events
of ch. vii. must come after ch. viii. and the Ammonite war
(x.–xii.).

round about, that the king said unto Nathan the prophet, **2**
See now, I dwell in an house of cedar, but the ark of God
dwelleth within curtains. And Nathan said to the king, **3**
Go, do all that is in thine heart; for the LORD is with thee.

4–17. *The Promise of the Permanence of David's Dynasty.*

Nathan at first encouraged David to build the Temple (*v.* 3).
Now a fresh message is entrusted to him. It may be thus
analysed: (1) Jehovah has always been satisfied to dwell in a
tent (*vv.* 6, 7); (2) He has dealt graciously with David (*vv.* 8, 9*a*);
(3) He will make him great (*v.* 9 *b*); (4) and will give Israel peace
(*vv.* 10, 11 *a*); (5) He will establish David's house for ever (*vv.*
11 *b*–16). This is an early form of the Messianic promise. The
hope is fixed upon an unbroken succession of prosperous kings
of David's line. The glories of the spiritual kingdom of 'great
David's greater Son' are not yet revealed. That vision must grow
slowly, as men gradually became able to grasp it.

And it came to pass the same night, that the word of the **4**
LORD came unto Nathan, saying, Go and tell my servant **5**
David, Thus saith the LORD, Shalt thou build me an
house for me to dwell in? for I have not dwelt in an **6**
house since the day that I brought up the children of
Israel out of Egypt, even to this day, but have walked in
a tent and in a tabernacle. In all places wherein I have **7**
walked with all the children of Israel, spake I a word
with any of the tribes of Israel, whom I commanded to
feed my people Israel, saying, Why have ye not built me
an house of cedar? Now therefore thus shalt thou say **8**
unto my servant David, Thus saith the LORD of hosts, I
took thee from the sheepcote, from following the sheep,
that thou shouldest be prince over my people, over Israel:
and I have been with thee whithersoever thou wentest, **9**
and have cut off all thine enemies from before thee; and
I will make thee a great name, like unto the name of the
great ones that are in the earth. And I will appoint a **10**

---

2. **Nathan the prophet**. He belongs to the great order of
prophets (not the dervish type), who preached righteousness to
Israel. He dared to rebuke the king's sin (xii. 7 ff.).

place for my people Israel, and will plant them, that they
may dwell in their own place, and be moved no more ;
neither shall the children of wickedness afflict them any
11 more, as at the first, and *as* from the day that I commanded judges to be over my people Israel ; and I will
cause thee to rest from all thine enemies. Moreover the
LORD telleth thee that the LORD will make thee an
12 house. When thy days be fulfilled, and thou shalt sleep
with thy fathers, I will set up thy seed after thee, which
shall proceed out of thy bowels, and I will establish his
13 kingdom. He shall build an house for my name, and I
14 will establish the throne of his kingdom for ever. I will
be his father, and he shall be my son : if he commit
iniquity, I will chasten him with the rod of men, and with
15 the stripes of the children of men ; but my mercy shall
not depart from him, as I took it from Saul, whom I put
16 away before thee. And thine house and thy kingdom
shall be made sure for ever before thee : thy throne
17 shall be established for ever. According to all these
words, and according to all this vision, so did Nathan
speak unto David.

18-29. *David's Answer.*

In this prayer David (1) thanks God humbly for His goodness
to him (*vv.* 18-21) ; (2) ascribes praise to Him for His dealings
with Israel (*vv.* 22-24) ; and (3) prays for the fulfilment of His
gracious promise (*vv.* 25-29).

18 Then David the king went in, and sat before the LORD ;
and he said, Who am I, O Lord GOD, and what is my

---

12 f. Refer specially to Solomon and the building of the
Temple.
14 f. Refer more generally to the Davidic line of kings. Each
king in turn would be Jehovah's son, guarded by His care and
chastened by His Fatherly love.
18. sat before the Lord. i.e. in the tent. The attitude of
sitting in prayer (peculiar to this passage) consisted probably of
sitting upon the heels, as Mohammedans do still.

house, that thou hast brought me thus far? And this 19
was yet a small thing in thine eyes, O Lord GOD; but
thou hast spoken also of thy servant's house for a great
while to come; and this *too* after the manner of men, O
Lord GOD! And what can David say more unto thee? 20
for thou knowest thy servant, O Lord GOD. For thy 21
word's sake, and according to thine own heart, hast thou
wrought all this greatness, to make thy servant know it.
Wherefore thou art great, O LORD God: for there is 22
none like thee, neither is there any God beside thee,
according to all that we have heard with our ears. And 23
what one nation in the earth is like thy people, even like
Israel, whom God went to redeem unto himself for a
people, and to make him a name, and to do great things
for you, and terrible things for thy land, before thy
people, which thou redeemedst to thee out of Egypt, *from*
the nations and their gods? And thou didst establish to 24
thyself thy people Israel to be a people unto thee for
ever; and thou, LORD, becamest their God. And now, 25
O LORD God, the word that thou hast spoken concerning
thy servant, and concerning his house, confirm thou it for
ever, and do as thou hast spoken. And let thy name be 26
magnified for ever, saying, The LORD of hosts is God
over Israel: and the house of thy servant David shall be
established before thee. For thou, O LORD of hosts, the 27
God of Israel, hast revealed to thy servant, saying, I will
build thee an house: therefore hath thy servant found in
his heart to pray this prayer unto thee. And now, O 28
Lord GOD, thou art God, and thy words are truth, and
thou hast promised this good thing unto thy servant:

---

19. after the manner of men. Condescending to my human
weakness and ambition. But the Heb., 'and this is the law of
man,' is of uncertain meaning, and perhaps corrupt.

23. for you. David can scarcely have addressed Israel in
the midst of his prayer to God. 1 Chr. xvii. 21 avoids this.

27. found in his heart. Lit. 'found his heart,' i.e. courage.
See marg. 'been bold.'

29 now therefore let it please thee to bless the house of thy
servant, that it may continue for ever before thee : for
thou, O Lord GOD, hast spoken it: and with thy blessing
let the house of thy servant be blessed for ever.

viii. 1-14. *Summary of David's Wars.*

8   And after this it came to pass, that David smote the
Philistines, and subdued them : and David took the
bridle of the mother city out of the hand of the Philis-
2 tines. And he smote Moab, and measured them with
the line, making them to lie down on the ground ; and he
measured two lines to put to death, and one full line to
keep alive. And the Moabites became servants to David,
3 and brought presents. David smote also Hadadezer the
son of Rehob, king of Zobah, as he went to recover his
4 dominion at the River. And David took from him a

(a) *Philistia* (*v.* 1).

viii. 1. And after this. Refers not to ch. vii. (see vii. 1 note),
but to what preceded in the original document from which the
compiler took the section, which he has worked up into its
present form.

   the bridle of the mother city. Probably, 'the power of con-
trol, or suzerainty, exercised by the chief city over the surround-
ing districts.' David became suzerain over Philistia on the west,
Edom on the south, Moab and Ammon on the east, and the
Syrian tribes on the north. Perhaps the text is corrupt.

(b) *Moab* (*v.* 2).

2. he measured two lines. Two-thirds of the male population were killed. Moab had probably aroused Israelite resentment
by aggressive behaviour during the civil war. The ban (see
Introd. p. xv.) was not fully carried out. The Chronicler
(1 Chron. xviii. 2) omits mention of the slaughter.

   brought presents. An acknowledgment of subjection.

(c) *Syria* (3-8).

The Syrian wars are also described in x. 6 ff. The Syrians
were first roused against David by the Ammonites. The allies
were defeated by Joab under the walls of Rabbath-Ammon ; and
afterwards Syria was conquered by David as far north as the river
Euphrates. It recovered its independence from Solomon.

3. Zobah. A Syrian state, lying north of Damascus.

   he went to recover &c. Read with 1 Chron. xviii. 3, 'as he

thousand and seven hundred horsemen, and twenty thousand footmen : and David houghed all the chariot horses, but reserved of them for an hundred chariots. And when 5 the Syrians of Damascus came to succour Hadadezer king of Zobah, David smote of the Syrians two and twenty thousand men. Then David put garrisons in Syria of 6 Damascus : and the Syrians became servants to David, and brought presents. And the LORD gave victory to David whithersoever he went. And David took the shields 7 of gold that were on the servants of Hadadezer, and brought them to Jerusalem. And from Betah and from 8 Berothai, cities of Hadadezer, king David took exceeding much brass. And when Toi king of Hamath heard that 9 David had smitten all the host of Hadadezer, then Toi 10 sent Joram his son unto king David, to salute him, and to bless him, because he had fought against Hadadezer and smitten him : for Hadadezer had wars with Toi. And *Joram* brought with him vessels of silver, and vessels of gold, and vessels of brass : these also did king David 11 dedicate unto the LORD, with the silver and gold that he dedicated of all the nations which he subdued ; of Syria, 12 and of Moab, and of the children of Ammon, and of the

---

went to establish his dominion &c.' The general hostility of the Syrians forced David to push his frontier to the Euphrates. Even from beyond that river forces were drawn to oppose him (x. 16 ff.). The Euphrates was regarded as Israel's northern boundary (see Deut. xi. 24), though only now did it actually reach so far north.

4. houghed (pronounced *hocked*). Lamed by cutting the back tendons of the hind leg, hamstrung.

5. Damascus. Supposed to be the oldest city in the world, afterwards the capital of Syria, Israel's powerful rival.

(*d*) *Embassy from Hamath* (9, 10).

9. Hamath. A kingdom north of Lebanon, and east of Zobah. The object of the embassy was to request peace.

(*e*) *David's Spoil* (11, 12).

12. of Syria. Or, ' Edom' (LXX); so Chron. In Hebrew the two names are very similar. See *v.* 13.

Philistines, and of Amalek, and of the spoil of Hadadezer,
13 son of Rehob, king of Zobah. And David gat him a
name when he returned from smiting of the Syrians in
14 the Valley of Salt, even eighteen thousand men. And he
put garrisons in Edom ; throughout all Edom put he
garrisons, and all the Edomites became servants to
David. And the LORD gave victory to David whithersoever he went.

15–18.   *David's Government.*

15   And David reigned over all Israel ; and David executed
16 judgement and justice unto all his people. And Joab the
son of Zeruiah was over the host ; and Jehoshaphat the
17 son of Ahilud was recorder : and Zadok the son of Ahitub,
and Ahimelech the son of Abiathar, were priests ; and
18 Seraiah was scribe ; and Benaiah the son of Jehoiada
was over the Cherethites and the Pelethites ; and David's
sons were priests.

(*f*)   *Edom* (13, 14).

13.   the Syrians. Heb. 'Aram.' Almost certainly we must
read 'Edom,' with LXX and 1 Chron. xviii. 12.

the Valley of Salt. On the southern frontier of Israel,
separating it from Edom. The Syrians could not be so far
south. Amaziah fought a great battle there (2 Kings xiv. 7)
against Edom. According to 1 Kings xi. 15 f. the ban was
executed upon Edom.

15.   executed judgement and justice. In a country just
emerging from semi-barbarism, where the wealthy and strong
alone had rights, a king who would 'judge his people with
righteousness, defend the poor, and punish the wrongdoer,' must
have seemed indeed God's representative.

16.   recorder. A minister who kept the account of business
to be done, or Grand Vizier.

17.   Zadok &c.   The names are in wrong order. It must
mean, 'Abiathar, the son of Ahimelech, the son of Ahitub (see
1 Sam. xxii. 20), and Zadok were priests.' See xv. 24. Abiathar
was one of David's earliest followers ; he joined him after Saul's
slaughter of the priests at Nob ; he was banished by Solomon for
his share in Adonijah's conspiracy (1 Kings ii. 26).

scribe. Secretary of State.

18.   Cherethites and Pelethites. The foreign body-guard.

C. The Court Record. IX.–XX.

These chapters, which are from a document of extreme antiquity (Introd. p. ix.), describe a series of events in the inner life of David's Court, during the 33 years after the capture of Jerusalem. The author was probably one who took part in them. Abiathar and Nathan have each been suggested.

(a) ix. *Ziba and Mephibosheth.*

And David said, Is there yet any that is left of the 9 house of Saul, that I may shew him kindness for Jonathan's sake? And there was of the house of Saul a servant 2 whose name was Ziba, and they called him unto David; and the king said unto him, Art thou Ziba? And he said, Thy servant is he. And the king said, Is there not 3 yet any of the house of Saul, that I may shew the kindness of God unto him? And Ziba said unto the king, Jonathan hath yet a son, which is lame on his feet. And the king said unto him, Where is he? And Ziba said 4 unto the king, Behold, he is in the house of Machir the son of Ammiel, in Lo-debar. Then king David sent, 5 and fetched him out of the house of Machir the son of Ammiel, from Lo-debar. And Mephibosheth, the son of 6 Jonathan, the son of Saul, came unto David, and fell on

---

The Cherethites were a Philistine tribe, lying S. of Judah (see 1 Sam. xxx. 14). 'Pelethites' is probably the same word as 'Philistines.'

David's sons were priests. Marg., 'chief ministers,' follows the LXX.

ix. 1. And David said. Evidently not the beginning of the document. See note on viii. 1.

for Jonathan's sake. In memory of the solemn and touching oath the two friends had sworn (1 Sam. xx. 14 ff.).

3. the kindness of God. Such as God shews, generous and undeserved. Such were the terms of the oath.

which is lame. See iv. 4.

4. Machir. A chief of the tribe of Manasseh in Gilead. During Absalom's rebellion he gave substantial help to David at Mahanaim (xvii. 27).

his face, and did obeisance. And David said, Mephibo-
7 sheth. And he answered, Behold thy servant! And
David said unto him, Fear not: for I will surely shew
thee kindness for Jonathan thy father's sake, and will
restore thee all the land of Saul thy father; and thou
8 shalt eat bread at my table continually. And he did
obeisance, and said, What is thy servant, that thou
9 shouldest look upon such a dead dog as I am? Then
the king called to Ziba, Saul's servant, and said unto him,
All that pertained to Saul and to all his house have I
10 given unto thy master's son. And thou shalt till the land
for him, thou, and thy sons, and thy servants; and thou
shalt bring in *the fruits*, that thy master's son may have
bread to eat: but Mephibosheth thy master's son shall
eat bread alway at my table. Now Ziba had fifteen sons
11 and twenty servants. Then said Ziba unto the king,
According to all that my lord the king commandeth his
servant, so shall thy servant do. As for Mephibosheth,
said the king, he shall eat at my table, as one of the
12 king's sons. And Mephibosheth had a young son, whose
name was Mica. And all that dwelt in the house of Ziba
13 were servants unto Mephibosheth. So Mephibosheth
dwelt in Jerusalem: for he did eat continually at the
king's table; and he was lame on both his feet.

---

7. Fear not. A new dynasty often established itself by
killing all the relatives of the late king. Cf. Jehu, 2 Kings x.
It was prudent to keep a living representative of Saul's house
under supervision; but David's treatment of this prince was
honourable and generous.

the land of Saul. At Gibeah. It had become David's (xii. 8).

8. a dead dog. Loathsome and contemptible. See note on
iii. 8.

10. And thou shalt till. Ziba was already tenant; but now
Mephibosheth, not David, was to be his landlord. The expense
of keeping up an establishment at Jerusalem would be considerable.

(b) x.–xii.   *The Ammonite War and David's Sin.*

x. 1–5.   *The Ammonite Outrage.*

And it came to pass after this, that the king of the 10 children of Ammon died, and Hanun his son reigned in his stead. And David said, I will shew kindness unto 2 Hanun the son of Nahash, as his father shewed kindness unto me. So David sent by the hand of his servants to comfort him concerning his father. And David's servants came into the land of the children of Ammon. But the 3 princes of the children of Ammon said unto Hanun their lord, Thinkest thou that David doth honour thy father, that he hath sent comforters unto thee? hath not David sent his servants unto thee to search the city, and to spy it out, and to overthrow it? So Hanun took David's 4 servants, and shaved off the one half of their beards, and cut off their garments in the middle, even to their buttocks, and sent them away. When they told it unto David, he 5 sent to meet them; for the men were greatly ashamed. And the king said, Tarry at Jericho until your beards be grown, and then return.

6–14.   *First Campaign against Ammon and Syria.*

And when the children of Ammon saw that they were 6 become odious to David, the children of Ammon sent and hired the Syrians of Beth-rehob, and the Syrians of

---

x. 2   Nahash. Saul's first foe (1 Sam. xi.).

3   the city. Rabbah, the capital. These foolish princes may have been alarmed at the overthrow of Moab (viii. 2), their neighbour.

4.   David's servants. The persons of ambassadors are sacred. This insult was especially brutal. The beard is with Orientals the symbol of manhood.

6.   the Syrians. These tribes lay north and north-east of Israel. On regaining their independence from Solomon (1 Kings xi. 23 ff.) they formed themselves into a powerful kingdom ith Damascus as their capital. They waged constant war with

Zobah, twenty thousand footmen, and the king of Maacah
with a thousand men, and the men of Tob twelve thou-
7 sand men.   And when David heard of it, he sent Joab,
8 and all the host of the mighty men.   And the children of
Ammon came out, and put the battle in array at the
entering in of the gate : and the Syrians of Zobah, and of
Rehob, and the men of Tob and Maacah, were by them-
9 selves in the field.   Now when Joab saw that the battle
was set against him before and behind, he chose of all
the choice men of Israel, and put them in array against
10 the Syrians : and the rest of the people he committed
into the hand of Abishai his brother, and he put them in
11 array against the children of Ammon.   And he said, If
the Syrians be too strong for me, then thou shalt help
me : but if the children of Ammon be too strong for thee,
12 then I will come and help thee.   Be of good courage, and
let us play the men for our people, and for the cities of
our God : and the LORD do that which seemeth him
13 good.   So Joab and the people that were with him drew
nigh unto the battle against the Syrians : and they fled
14 before him.   And when the children of Ammon saw that

Israel, until their power was broken by Assyria.   Zobah seems
to have been the most considerable of the confederates ; in Saul's
time there were 'kings of Zobah' (1 Sam. xiv. 47) ; now these
chiefs were combined under one king, Hadadezer.   •

8 ff.   The Ammonites gave battle just outside the gate of the
city (probably Rabbah).   Their Syrian allies were lying in am-
bush at some distance.   The design was to catch Joab between
two forces.   Joab however detected the scheme and divided his
army.   With a body of picked troops he hurled himself against
the Syrians (probably the more dangerous enemy), whom he defeated.   Abishai, with the main army, attacked the Ammonites.
These, discouraged by the overthrow of their allies, were driven
into their city.   The season being too late for a siege, Joab
returned to Jerusalem.

12.   for the cities of our God.   But this was not a defensive
war.   'For the Ark of God' has been suggested.   The Ark was
in the camp (xi. 11) ; it was the symbol of His Presence ; and
they were His troops fighting His battles against His foes.

the Syrians were fled, they likewise fled before Abishai,
and entered into the city. Then Joab returned from the
children of Ammon, and came to Jerusalem.

15-19. *Syrian Wars.*

This passage, which describes the same events as viii. 3-8, has
probably been inserted between x. 14 and xi. 1.

And when the Syrians saw that they were put to the 15
worse before Israel, they gathered themselves together.
And Hadarezer sent, and brought out the Syrians that 16
were beyond the River: and they came to Helam, with
Shobach the captain of the host of Hadarezer at their
head. And it was told David; and he gathered all 17
Israel together, and passed over Jordan, and came to
Helam. And the Syrians set themselves in array against
David, and fought with him. And the Syrians fled before 18
Israel; and David slew of the Syrians *the men of* seven
hundred chariots, and forty thousand horsemen, and
smote Shobach the captain of their host, that he died
there. And when all the kings that were servants to 19
Hadarezer saw that they were put to the worse before
Israel, they made peace with Israel, and served them.
So the Syrians feared to help the children of Ammon any
more.

xi. 1.   *The Siege of Rabbah.*

And it came to pass, at the return of the year, at the 11
time when kings go out *to battle*, that David sent Joab,
and his servants with him, and all Israel; and they
destroyed the children of Ammon, and besieged Rabbah.
But David tarried at Jerusalem.

---

16. Hadarezer. Hadadezer (viii. 3) is the right spelling.

the Syrians that were beyond the River, i.e. the Euphrates.
In viii. 5 these are 'the Syrians of Damascus.'

xi. 1. Next spring Joab renewed the war against Ammon.
Devastating the country as he advanced, he marched with the
guards and the Israelite militia upon Rabbah, which he besieged.

2-5. *David's Sin.*

2   And it came to pass at eventide, that David arose from
off his bed, and walked upon the roof of the king's house :
and from the roof he saw a woman bathing ; and the
3 woman was very beautiful to look upon.   And David sent
and inquired after the woman.   And one said, Is not this
Bath-sheba, the daughter of Eliam, the wife of Uriah the
4 Hittite?   And David sent messengers, and took her ;
and she came in unto him, and he lay with her ; (for she
was purified from her uncleanness ;) and she returned
5 unto her house.   And the woman conceived ; and she
sent and told David, and said, I am with child.

6-13. *Uriah sent from the Camp.*

6 And David sent to Joab, *saying*, Send me Uriah the
7 Hittite.   And Joab sent Uriah to David.   And when
Uriah was come unto him, David asked of him how Joab
did, and how the people fared, and how the war prospered.
8 And David said to Uriah, Go down to thy house, and
wash thy feet.   And Uriah departed out of the king's
house, and there followed him a mess *of meat* from the
9 king.   But Uriah slept at the door of the king's house
with all the servants of his lord, and went not down to
10 his house.   And when they had told David, saying, Uriah
went not down unto his house, David said unto Uriah,
Art thou not come from a journey? wherefore didst thou
11 not go down unto thine house?   And Uriah said unto

---

2. from off his bed.   From his midday rest ; a common
custom in hot countries (see iv. 5).

the roof.   Roofs in the East are flat, and much used.

3. Eliam.   One of David's Order of the Thirty, and son of
Ahithophel (xxiii. 34).

Uriah.   A foreigner, also of the Thirty (*ib.* 39).

9. But Uriah slept.   David's scheme for hiding his sin was
defeated by Uriah's punctiliousness.   A soldier on active service,
being consecrated, might not enter an ordinary house.   Uriah
would not visit his.

David, The ark, and Israel, and Judah, abide in booths ; and my lord Joab, and the servants of my lord, are encamped in the open field ; shall I then go into mine house, to eat and to drink, and to lie with my wife? as thou livest, and as thy soul liveth, I will not do this thing. And David said to Uriah, Tarry here to-day also, and 12 to-morrow I will let thee depart. So Uriah abode in Jerusalem that day, and the morrow. And when David 13 had called him, he did eat and drink before him ; and he made him drunk : and at even he went out to lie on his bed with the servants of his lord, but went not down to his house.

14–17. *The Murder of Uriah.*

And it came to pass in the morning, that David wrote a 14 letter to Joab, and sent it by the hand of Uriah. And he 15 wrote in the letter, saying, Set ye Uriah in the forefront of the hottest battle, and retire ye from him, that he may be smitten, and die. And it came to pass, when Joab 16 kept watch upon the city, that he assigned Uriah unto the place where he knew that valiant men were. And the 17 men of the city went out, and fought with Joab . and there fell some of the people, even of the servants of David ; and Uriah the Hittite died also.

18–25. *Joab's Despatch.*

Then Joab sent and told David all the things concerning 18 the war ; and he charged the messenger, saying, When 19 thou hast made an end of telling all the things concerning the war unto the king, it shall be that, if the king's wrath 20 arise, and he say unto thee, Wherefore went ye so nigh unto the city to fight? knew ye not that they would shoot

---

11.   The ark.   See note on x. 12.
16.   he assigned Uriah.   Joab had no scruple in carrying out David's infamous command, though he had great regard for the ceremonial customs of religion.   Cf. xxiv. 3.

21 from the wall? who smote Abimelech the son of Jerubbesheth? did not a woman cast an upper millstone upon
him from the wall, that he died at Thebez? why went ye
so nigh the wall? then shalt thou say, Thy servant Uriah
22 the Hittite is dead also. So the messenger went, and
came and shewed David all that Joab had sent him for.
23 And the messenger said unto David, The men prevailed
against us, and came out unto us into the field, and we
24 were upon them even unto the entering of the gate. And
the shooters shot at thy servants from off the wall; and
some of the king's servants be dead, and thy servant
25 Uriah the Hittite is dead also. Then David said unto
the messenger, Thus shalt thou say unto Joab, Let not
this thing displease thee, for the sword devoureth one as
well as another: make thy battle more strong against the
city, and overthrow it: and encourage thou him.

26, 27. *Bath-sheba made David's Wife.*

26 And when the wife of Uriah heard that Uriah her husband
27 was dead, she made lamentation for her husband. And
when the mourning was past, David sent and took her
home to his house, and she became his wife, and bare him
a son. But the thing that David had done displeased the
LORD.

xii. 1-6. *Nathan's Parable.*

12 And the LORD sent Nathan unto David. And he
came unto him, and said unto him, There were two men

---

21. Abimelech. See Judg. ix. 50 ff.
Jerubbesheth. Jerubbaal or Gideon (Judg. vi. 32). For the
disguise in the name, cf. ii. 8 note.
27. David sent &c. Though he had been guilty of adultery,
hypocrisy and murder, he was not unhappy. We are taught here
how even a good man may fall into terrible sin, and how one sin
leads to another, hardening the heart and blinding the conscience.
Yet God does not leave sinners without warning (as ch. xii.
shews), but on repentance He forgives.
xii. 1. the Lord sent Nathan. If David had forgotten his sin,

in one city; the one rich, and the other poor. The rich 2
man had exceeding many flocks and herds: but the poor 3
man had nothing, save one little ewe lamb, which he had
bought and nourished up: and it grew up together with
him, and with his children; it did eat of his own morsel,
and drank of his own cup, and lay in his bosom, and was
unto him as a daughter. And there came a traveller unto 4
the rich man, and he spared to take of his own flock and
of his own herd, to dress for the wayfaring man that was
come unto him, but took the poor man's lamb, and dressed
it for the man that was come to him. And David's anger 5
was greatly kindled against the man; and he said to
Nathan, As the LORD liveth, the man that hath done this
is worthy to die: and he shall restore the lamb fourfold, 6
because he did this thing, and because he had no pity.

7-14. *David's Confession and Forgiveness.*

And Nathan said to David, Thou art the man. Thus 7
saith the LORD, the God of Israel, I anointed thee king
over Israel, and I delivered thee out of the hand of Saul;
and I gave thee thy master's house, and thy master's 8
wives into thy bosom, and gave thee the house of Israel
and of Judah; and if that had been too little, I would
have added unto thee such and such things. Wherefore 9
hast thou despised the word of the LORD, to do that
which is evil in his sight? thou hast smitten Uriah the

God had not. Nathan was a prophet in the highest sense (vii. 2),
not only foretelling events (as he did, see *v.* 14), but more especially
declaring God's Will. By a parable he convicted the king of
mean selfishness and heartless injustice.

6. fourfold. So the law ordered, Ex. xxii. 1. Cf. Zaccheus
(Lc. xix. 8). The LXX has ' sevenfold.'

7. Thou art the man. David had unsuspectingly condemned
his own evil acts. The boldness of the prophet and the humility
of the king are both admirable.

9. evil in his sight. The sin was against God more than
against man. David had flouted the authority of the Supreme

Hittite with the sword, and hast taken his wife to be thy wife, and hast slain him with the sword of the children of 10 Ammon. Now therefore, the sword shall never depart from thine house; because thou hast despised me, and hast taken the wife of Uriah the Hittite to be thy wife. 11 Thus saith the LORD, Behold, I will raise up evil against thee out of thine own house, and I will take thy wives before thine eyes, and give them unto thy neighbour, and 12 he shall lie with thy wives in the sight of this sun. For thou didst it secretly: but I will do this thing before all 13 Israel, and before the sun. And David said unto Nathan, I have sinned against the LORD. And Nathan said unto David, The LORD also hath put away thy sin; thou shalt 14 not die. Howbeit, because by this deed thou hast given great occasion to the enemies of the LORD to blaspheme, 15 the child also that is born unto thee shall surely die. And Nathan departed unto his house.

15–23. *The Child's Death.*

And the LORD struck the child that Uriah's wife bare 16 unto David, and it was very sick. David therefore besought God for the child; and David fasted, and went in, 17 and lay all night upon the earth. And the elders of his house arose, *and stood* beside him, to raise him up from the earth: but he would not, neither did he eat bread with 18 them. And it came to pass on the seventh day, that the

King and had repaid with ingratitude the unprecedented favours he had received.

10 ff. The rest of the Court Record is the history of the fulfilment of this prediction.

14. Howbeit, because by this deed &c. Forgiveness does not bring immunity from the effects of sin. David, in submitting to this penance, perfected his penitence.

16. David fasted. In heathen religions fasting is meant to move the pity or avert the envy of the gods. With Jews and Christians it is an expression of penitence.

The tenses here used (frequentative) shew that David prayed, fasted and watched for the whole seven days.

child died. And the servants of David feared to tell him that the child was dead: for they said, Behold, while the child was yet alive, we spake unto him, and he hearkened not unto our voice: how will he then vex himself, if we tell him that the child is dead? But when David saw 19 that his servants whispered together, David perceived that the child was dead: and David said unto his servants, Is the child dead? And they said, He is dead. Then 20 David arose from the earth, and washed, and anointed himself, and changed his apparel; and he came into the house of the LORD, and worshipped: then he came to his own house; and when he required they set bread before him, and he did eat. Then said his servants unto him, 21 What thing is this that thou hast done? thou didst fast and weep for the child, while it was alive; but when the child was dead, thou didst rise and eat bread. And he 22 said, While the child was yet alive, I fasted and wept: for I said, Who knoweth whether the LORD will not be gracious to me, that the child may live? But now he is 23 dead, wherefore should I fast? can I bring him back again? I shall go to him, but he shall not return to me.

24, 25. *The Birth of Solomon.*

And David comforted Bath-sheba his wife, and went in 24 unto her, and lay with her: and she bare a son, and he called his name Solomon. And the LORD loved him; and 25

---

20. washed &c. The marks of mourning are put off; marks of joy are put on.

23. I shall go to him. David regarded the child as still alive in Sheol (Hades), but with a vague shadowy existence. Cf. Hezekiah's thoughts of death, Is. xxxviii. 18. See Introd. p. xiv.

24. Solomon. The name (= 'Peaceful') is explained in 1 Chron. xxii. 9 as given because his reign should be peaceful, not full of wars as David's had been.

25. the Lord loved him. A striking instance of God's electing love. As He had chosen David, the youngest of his family, and Jacob, not the elder brother Esau, so now He chose the youngest of David's sons.

he sent by the hand of Nathan the prophet, and he called
his name Jedidiah, for the LORD'S sake.

26–31.   *Conquest of Ammon.*

26   Now Joab fought against Rabbah of the children of
27 Ammon, and took the royal city.   And Joab sent messengers to David, and said, I have fought against Rabbah,
28 yea, I have taken the city of waters.   Now therefore
gather the rest of the people together, and encamp
against the city, and take it : lest I take the city, and it
29 be called after my name.   And David gathered all the
people together, and went to Rabbah, and fought against
30 it, and took it.   And he took the crown of their king from
off his head ; and the weight thereof was a talent of gold,
and *in it were* precious stones ; and it was set on David's
head.   And he brought forth the spoil of the city, exceed-
31 ing much.   And he brought forth the people that were
therein, and put them under saws, and under harrows of
iron, and under axes of iron, and made them pass
through the brickkiln : and thus did he unto all the cities
of the children of Ammon.   And David and all the people
returned unto Jerusalem.

---

26 f.   The commencement of this campaign is described in xi. 1.
Rabbah was a strongly fortified city, with a fort to guard the water
supply.   This fort was 'the city of waters' that Joab took, making the main city untenable.   In 218 B.C. Antiochus Epiphanes
captured this same city by stopping the water supply.

28.   lest I take the city.   Joab's self-denying loyalty is beyond
praise.

30.   their king.   Better, 'Milcom,' the Ammonite deity.   The
crown (weighing 54 lbs. at least) was too heavy for the head of
the king, but might have adorned the head of an idol.

precious stones.   Rather, 'one stone of special value' (LXX).
This was taken out of the crown to be worn by David.

31.   put them under saws &c.   Either David tortured and
slew his enemies in this way (as the text), or (slightly altering
the Heb. with marg.) 'he set them to forced labour with saws,
iron picks and axes, and at the brick-mould.'

(c)   xiii., xiv.   *Amnon's Crime and Absalom's Revenge.*

xiii. 1-22.   *Amnon's Crime.*

With this chapter begins the working out of the tragedy of David's family history, the nemesis of his own sin (xii. 10 ff.). The lax morality of the Eastern harem, instituted by David, found a signal expression in Amnon's crime, Absalom's fierce revenge, and finally in the formidable rebellion of that prince against his father. The present chapter throws light on the domestic customs of high life in Jerusalem.

And it came to pass after this, that Absalom the son of 13 David had a fair sister, whose name was Tamar; and Amnon the son of David loved her. And Amnon was 2 so vexed that he fell sick because of his sister Tamar; for she was a virgin; and it seemed hard to Amnon to do any thing unto her. But Amnon had a friend, whose 3 name was Jonadab, the son of Shimeah David's brother: and Jonadab was a very subtil man. And he said unto 4 him, Why, O son of the king, art thou thus lean from day to day? wilt thou not tell me? And Amnon said unto him, I love Tamar, my brother Absalom's sister. And 5 Jonadab said unto him, Lay thee down on thy bed, and feign thyself sick: and when thy father cometh to see thee, say unto him, Let my sister Tamar come, I pray thee, and give me bread to eat, and dress the food in my sight, that I may see it, and eat it at her hand. So 6 Amnon lay down, and feigned himself sick: and when

---

xiii. 1. Absalom. Son of David and Maacah, the princess of Geshur (iii. 3). He was beautiful and charming, but fierce, unforgiving, unprincipled, remorseless and ambitious. **Tamar.** His sister by the same mother. **Amnon.** Half-brother to Absalom and Tamar.

2. he fell sick. The Semites are a strongly emotional race : far more passionate in love, hatred, and revenge than Englishmen are.

it seemed hard. Unmarried women of the upper classes were kept in seclusion.

3. Jonadab. A type of evil friendship and perverted cleverness.

the king was come to see him, Amnon said unto the
king, Let my sister Tamar come, I pray thee, and make
me a couple of cakes in my sight, that I may eat at her
7 hand.   Then David sent home to Tamar, saying, Go now
8 to thy brother Amnon's house, and dress him food.   So
Tamar went to her brother Amnon's house; and he was
laid down.   And she took dough, and kneaded it, and
9 made cakes in his sight, and did bake the cakes.   And
she took the pan, and poured them out before him; but
he refused to eat.   And Amnon said, Have out all men
10 from me.   And they went out every man from him.   And
Amnon said unto Tamar, Bring the food into the chamber,
that I may eat of thine hand.   And Tamar took the cakes
which she had made, and brought them into the chamber
11 to Amnon her brother.   And when she had brought them
near unto him to eat, he took hold of her, and said unto
12 her, Come lie with me, my sister.   And she answered
him, Nay, my brother, do not force me; for no such thing
13 ought to be done in Israel: do not thou this folly.   And
I, whither shall I carry my shame? and as for thee, thou
shalt be as one of the fools in Israel.   Now therefore, I
pray thee, speak unto the king; for he will not withhold
14 me from thee.   Howbeit he would not hearken unto her
voice: but being stronger than she, he forced her, and lay
15 with her.   Then Amnon hated her with exceeding great
hatred; for the hatred wherewith he hated her was
greater than the love wherewith he had loved her.   And

---

8. she took dough &c.   The ladies of Jerusalem were
acquainted with the domestic arts.

12. no such thing ought to be done in Israel.   Better, 'it
is not wont so to be done.'   There is a difference between
Jehovah's people and the heathen: *noblesse oblige.*   A strong
regard for custom is characteristic of the East.

folly.   Bad behaviour, immorality.

13. he will not withhold me.   Such marriages were permitted in early times.   Sarah was half-sister to Abraham (Gen. xx.
12).   They were forbidden later (see Lev. xviii. 9).

Amnon said unto her, Arise, be gone. And she said unto 16
him, Not so, because this great wrong in putting me forth
is *worse* than the other that thou didst unto me. But he
would not hearken unto her. Then he called his servant 17
that ministered unto him, and said, Put now this woman
out from me, and bolt the door after her. And she had a 18
garment of divers colours upon her: for with such robes
were the king's daughters that were virgins apparelled.
Then his servant brought her out, and bolted the door
after her. And Tamar put ashes on her head, and rent 19
her garment of divers colours that was on her ; and she
laid her hand on her head, and went her way, crying
aloud as she went. And Absalom her brother said unto 20
her, Hath Amnon thy brother been with thee? but now
hold thy peace, my sister: he is thy brother; take not
this thing to heart. So Tamar remained desolate in her
brother Absalom's house. But when king David heard of 21
all these things, he was very wroth. And Absalom spake 22
unto Amnon neither good nor bad: for Absalom hated
Amnon, because he had forced his sister Tamar.

23–29. *Absalom's Revenge.*

And it came to pass after two full years, that Absalom 23
had sheepshearers in Baal-hazor, which is beside Ephraim:
and Absalom invited all the king's sons. And Absalom 24
came to the king, and said, Behold now, thy servant hath

---

18. garment of divers colours. Probably (with marg.) a
long garment with sleeves reaching to the feet. Joseph wore
such a garment (Gen. xxxvii. 3).

21. he was very wroth. Yet did not punish Amnon. This
weakness, so disastrous in its results, is emphasised as one of
David's worst defects. Cf. 1 Kings i. 6, and his treatment of
Absalom. It was also Eli's great fault (1 Sam. iii. 13).

23. two full years. Absalom's revenge was a deliberate act,
not an impulse of ferocity. By the delay he hoped to disarm
Amnon's fears.

sheepshearers. The sheep-shearing was a festival marked by
sacrifice and merry-making.

sheepshearers; let the king, I pray thee, and his servants
25 go with thy servant. And the king said to Absalom, Nay,
my son, let us not all go, lest we be burdensome unto
thee. And he pressed him: howbeit he would not go,
26 but blessed him. Then said Absalom, If not, I pray thee,
let my brother Amnon go with us. And the king said
27 unto him, Why should he go with thee? But Absalom
pressed him, that he let Amnon and all the king's sons go
28 with him. And Absalom commanded his servants, saying,
Mark ye now, when Amnon's heart is merry with wine;
and when I say unto you, Smite Amnon, then kill him,
fear not: have not I commanded you? be courageous,
29 and be valiant. And the servants of Absalom did unto
Amnon as Absalom had commanded. Then all the king's
sons arose, and every man gat him up upon his mule, and
fled.

30-37. *David receives the News.*

30 And it came to pass, while they were in the way, that the
tidings came to David, saying, Absalom hath slain all the
31 king's sons, and there is not one of them left.   Then the
king arose, and rent his garments, and lay on the earth;
and all his servants stood by with their clothes rent.
32 And Jonadab, the son of Shimeah David's brother,
answered and said, Let not my lord suppose that they
have killed all the young men the king's sons; for Amnon
only is dead: for by the appointment of Absalom this
hath been determined from the day that he forced his
33 sister Tamar.   Now therefore let not my lord the king

---

26. let my brother. Amnon, the eldest, as David's representative.   David evidently was anxious, but did not refuse.

32. Jonadab. Amnon's clever friend shewed small regret for
him, though his death was the result of his own advice.

by the appointment &c. Some read, 'upon the mouth (face)
of Absalom there hath been a scowl since the day &c.'   Graphic,
but not likely in one who, being an expert dissembler, wished to
disarm suspicion.

take the thing to his heart, to think that all the king's sons are dead: for Amnon only is dead. But Absalom 34 fled. And the young man that kept the watch lifted up his eyes, and looked, and, behold, there came much people by the way of the hill side behind him. And 35 Jonadab said unto the king, Behold, the king's sons are come: as thy servant said, so it is. And it came to pass, 36 as soon as he had made an end of speaking, that, behold, the king's sons came, and lifted up their voice, and wept: and the king also and all his servants wept very sore. But Absalom fled, and went to Talmai the son of Ammihur, 37 king of Geshur. And *David* mourned for his son every day.

38, 39. *Absalom's Exile.*

So Absalom fled, and went to Geshur, and was there 38 three years. And *the soul of* king David longed to go 39 forth unto Absalom: for he was comforted concerning Amnon, seeing he was dead.

xiv. 1–24. *The Wise Woman of Tekoa.*

Now Joab the son of Zeruiah perceived that the king's 14 heart was toward Absalom. And Joab sent to Tekoa, 2 and fetched thence a wise woman, and said unto her,

---

39. the soul of king David. If he longed to recall him it is not easy to see why he did not. The Vulgate has, 'cessavitque rex David persequi Absalom'; he gave up his plan of pursuit and revenge. The text is probably corrupt.

xiv. 1. the king's heart was toward Absalom. Either his natural affection was strengthened by lapse of time and absence, so that Joab saw that the moment was propitious for effecting a reconciliation, or (reading 'against' for 'toward') the king was still indignant at this revival of the old custom of private revenge, which he was trying to stamp out; in which case, Joab, who would sympathise with Absalom, felt he must intervene.

2. Tekoa. Twelve miles south of Jerusalem. It was the home of the prophet Amos.

a wise woman. One possessing unusual, probably magical, skill. Shakespeare's 'wise woman of Brentford' was a witch.

I pray thee, feign thyself to be a mourner, and put on mourning apparel, I pray thee, and anoint not thyself with oil, but be as a woman that had a long time mourned
3 for the dead: and go in to the king, and speak on this manner unto him. So Joab put the words in her mouth.
4 And when the woman of Tekoa spake to the king, she fell on her face to the ground, and did obeisance, and said,
5 Help, O king. And the king said unto her, What aileth thee? And she answered, Of a truth I am a widow
6 woman, and mine husband is dead. And thy handmaid had two sons, and they two strove together in the field, and there was none to part them, but the one smote the
7 other, and killed him. And, behold, the whole family is risen against thine handmaid, and they said, Deliver him that smote his brother, that we may kill him for the life of his brother whom he slew, and so destroy the heir also: thus shall they quench my coal which is left, and shall leave to my husband neither name nor remainder upon the
8 face of the earth. And the king said unto the woman, Go to thine house, and I will give charge concerning thee.
9 And the woman of Tekoa said unto the king, My lord, O king, the iniquity be on me, and on my father's house:
o and the king and his throne be guiltless. And the king said, Whosoever saith aught unto thee, bring him to me,
1 and he shall not touch thee any more. Then said she, I pray thee, let the king remember the LORD thy God, that the avenger of blood destroy not any more, lest they

---

3. go in to the king. Justice was a simple matter in those days. See Introd. p. xii.

7. And, behold. By the law of blood-revenge, the tribe was bound to kill one who had shed the blood of a tribesman. The duty was delegated to one who was called 'the avenger of blood' (*v.* 11). As Joab knew, David, who wished to bring all justice into his own hand, would entirely sympathise with this plea.

quench my coal. So long as one coal is alive, the fire may be rekindled. If her only son were killed, her hope of descendants would be extinguished.

destroy my son. And he said, As the LORD liveth, there
shall not one hair of thy son fall to the earth. Then the 12
woman said, Let thine handmaid, I pray thee, speak a
word unto my lord the king. And he said, Say on. And 13
the woman said, Wherefore then hast thou devised such
a thing against the people of God? for in speaking this
word the king is as one which is guilty, in that the king
doth not fetch home again his banished one. For we 14
must needs die, and are as water spilt on the ground,
which cannot be gathered up again; neither doth God
take away life, but deviseth means, that he that is banished
be not an outcast from him. Now therefore seeing that 15
I am come to speak this word unto my lord the king, it is
because the people have made me afraid: and thy handmaid said, I will now speak unto the king; it may be
that the king will perform the request of his servant.
For the king will hear, to deliver his servant out of the 16
hand of the man that would destroy me and my son
together out of the inheritance of God. Then thine 17
handmaid said, Let, I pray thee, the word of my lord
the king be comfortable: for as an angel of God, so is
my lord the king to discern good and bad: and the LORD

---

13. the king is as one which is guilty. Like Nathan (ch. xii.),
she turns her case to shew David, as in a mirror, the meaning of
his own action. If he is right in extending mercy to her son, he
must be wrong in refusing it to his own, and so wronging 'the
people of God' by banishing the heir to the throne.

14. The meaning seems to be: (1) Life, once gone, is beyond
recall; but (2) Jehovah is not in favour of banishing His worshippers from the land where they serve Him; that would be
to lose their worship. So He brings them back after a term
of exile. This had been David's experience in earlier life. So,
Amnon being dead, no harshness to Absalom can recall him;
but let the king deal mercifully with Absalom, as Jehovah deals
with His exiles.

16. the inheritance of God. The land of Israel. Death
before Christ was not gain, but destruction out of God's inheritance. See Introd. p. xiv.

17. to discern good and bad. To judge between right and
wrong.

H.   4

18 thy God be with thee. Then the king answered and said
unto the woman, Hide not from me, I pray thee, aught
that I shall ask thee. And the woman said, Let my lord
19 the king now speak. And the king said, Is the hand of
Joab with thee in all this? And the woman answered and
said, As thy soul liveth, my lord the king, none can turn
to the right hand or to the left from aught that my lord
the king hath spoken: for thy servant Joab, he bade me,
and he put all these words in the mouth of thine hand-
20 maid: to change the face of the matter hath thy servant
Joab done this thing: and my lord is wise, according to
the wisdom of an angel of God, to know all things that
21 are in the earth. And the king said unto Joab, Behold
now, I have done this thing: go therefore, bring the young
22 man Absalom again. And Joab fell to the ground on his
face, and did obeisance, and blessed the king: and Joab
said, To-day thy servant knoweth that I have found grace
in thy sight, my lord, O king, in that the king hath
23 performed the request of his servant. So Joab arose
and went to Geshur, and brought Absalom to Jerusalem.
24 And the king said, Let him turn to his own house, but
let him not see my face. So Absalom turned to his own
house, and saw not the king's face.

25-27. *Absalom's Beauty.*

25 Now in all Israel there was none to be so much praised
as Absalom for his beauty: from the sole of his foot even
to the crown of his head there was no blemish in him.
26 And when he polled his head, (now it was at every year's
end that he polled it: because *the hair* was heavy on him,
therefore he polled it:) he weighed the hair of his head at

---

20. to change the face of the matter. To alter the unpromis-
ing and uncomfortable relations between the king and the heir.

24. David was too weak to punish his son, or to forgive him
fully. Possibly Bathsheba's influence was working against
Absalom in favour of her son Solomon.

26. polled. Cut the hair of.

two hundred shekels, after the king's weight.   And unto 27
Absalom there were born three sons, and one daughter,
whose name was Tamar: she was a woman of a fair
countenance.

28-33.   *The Forgiveness of Absalom.*

And Absalom dwelt two full years in Jerusalem; and 28
he saw not the king's face.   Then Absalom sent for Joab, 29
to send him to the king; but he would not come to him:
and he sent again a second time, but he would not come.
Therefore he said unto his servants, See, Joab's field is 30
near mine, and he hath barley there; go and set it on fire.
And Absalom's servants set the field on fire.   Then Joab 31
arose, and came to Absalom unto his house, and said unto
him, Wherefore have thy servants set my field on fire?
And Absalom answered Joab, Behold, I sent unto thee, 32
saying, Come hither, that I may send thee to the king, to
say, Wherefore am I come from Geshur? it were better for
me to be there still: now therefore let me see the king's
face; and if there be iniquity in me, let him kill me.   So 33
Joab came to the king, and told him: and when he had
called for Absalom, he came to the king, and bowed
himself on his face to the ground before the king: and
the king kissed Absalom.

---

two hundred shekels.   Probably about 3½lbs.

the king's weight.   If 'the king'=the Persian monarch, this
passage must have been written during the Persian Supremacy
(533-333 B.C.).

27.   three sons.   See note on xviii. 18.

one daughter.   Tamar.   Cf. 1 Kings xv. 2, where she is
called Maacah.

29.   Absalom sent.   He was not free to roam at will.

he would not come.   Joab had probably by now some cause
for suspecting Absalom's loyalty; he was evidently no longer
willing to use his influence on his behalf.

30.   Joab's field &c.   He expected that Joab would come to
complain.   He wished to regain freedom, so that he might
pursue his ambitious schemes.

(d) xv.-xix. *Absalom's Rebellion.*

This vivid and detailed narrative falls into five stages: (1) xv. 1-12—Four years of plotting and preparation; (2) xv. 13-xvi. 14—David's flight from Jerusalem to Gilead; (3) xvi. 15-xvii. 29—Absalom's occupation of Jerusalem; (4) xviii. 1-xix. 8—The overthrow of the conspiracy; (5) xix. 9-43—David's home-coming.

xv. 1-6. *How Absalom duped the People.*

15 And it came to pass after this, that Absalom prepared him a chariot and horses, and fifty men to run before
2 him. And Absalom rose up early, and stood beside the way of the gate: and it was so, that when any man had a suit which should come to the king for judgement, then Absalom called unto him, and said, Of what city art thou? And he said, Thy servant is of one of the tribes of Israel.
3 And Absalom said unto him, See, thy matters are good and right; but there is no man deputed of the king to
4 hear thee. Absalom said moreover, Oh that I were made judge in the land, that every man which hath any suit or cause might come unto me, and I would do him justice!
5 And it was so, that when any man came nigh to do him obeisance, he put forth his hand, and took hold of him,
6 and kissed him. And on this manner did Absalom to all Israel that came to the king for judgement: so Absalom stole the hearts of the men of Israel.

---

xv. 1. after this. Being now free and apparently reconciled to David, Absalom began to sow the seeds of rebellion, (*a*) by assuming, as heir, royal state, chariot, horses and runners (see 1 Sam. viii. 11); (*b*) by courting the favour of the people. For four years he pursued this highly suspicious behaviour, yet David neither suspected nor checked him.

2. the way of the gate. The road leading to the palace gate. Public business was usually done about the gates. Cf. xix. 8.

4. Oh that I were made judge. Probably he did not ask to be made king instead of David, but that, as his deputy, he might attend to these many cases which the king could not personally attend to and which he would allow no one else to decide. There was probably a grievance, which Absalom made the most of. See Introd. p. xii.

6. stole the hearts of. Deceived. Cf. Gen. xxxi. 20 marg.

7–12. *The Outbreak of Rebellion.*

And it came to pass at the end of forty years, that 7
Absalom said unto the king, I pray thee, let me go and
pay my vow, which I have vowed unto the LORD, in
Hebron. For thy servant vowed a vow while I abode at 8
Geshur in Syria, saying, If the LORD shall indeed bring
me again to Jerusalem, then I will serve the LORD.
And the king said unto him, Go in peace. So he arose, 9
and went to Hebron. But Absalom sent spies through- 10
out all the tribes of Israel, saying, As soon as ye hear the
sound of the trumpet, then ye shall say, Absalom is king
in Hebron. And with Absalom went two hundred men 11
out of Jerusalem, that were invited, and went in their
simplicity; and they knew not any thing. And Absalom 12
sent for Ahithophel the Gilonite, David's counsellor, from
his city, even from Giloh, while he offered the sacrifices.
And the conspiracy was strong; for the people increased
continually with Absalom.

13–16. *Jerusalem evacuated.*

And there came a messenger to David, saying, The 13
hearts of the men of Israel are after Absalom. And 14
David said unto all his servants that were with him at

---

7. forty. A mistake for 'four' (marg.).

8. I will serve the Lord. By offering a solemn sacrifice to
God whom he thought of as having a special abode at Hebron.

9. Hebron. Chosen as (*a*) well-disposed to Absalom; he
was born there; (*b*) ill-disposed to David, who had transferred
his capital from Hebron to Jerusalem; (*c*) the chief town of Judah,
and jealous of the rest of Israel.

10. spies. Rather, 'secret messengers.'

11. two hundred men. They went merely as guests, but
finding themselves compromised, he hoped they would throw
their influence on the side of the conspiracy.

12. Ahithophel. David's chief counsellor, the father of
Eliam, and grandfather of Bathsheba (xi. 3, xxiii. 34). He had
cause to hate David.

sacrifices. Part of the coronation. Cf. 1 Sam. xi. 15.

14. his servants. The chief officials.

Jerusalem, Arise, and let us flee; for else none of us shall
escape from Absalom: make speed to depart, lest he
overtake us quickly, and bring down evil upon us, and
15 smite the city with the edge of the sword. And the
king's servants said unto the king, Behold, thy servants
are ready to do whatsoever my lord the king shall choose.
16 And the king went forth, and all his household after him.
And the king left ten women, which were concubines, to
keep the house.

17-23.   *The Passage of the Kidron.*

No twenty-four hours in Hebrew history are so fully and
graphically described as these that elapsed between David's flight
from Jerusalem and his crossing of the Jordan (xvii. 22).

17 And the king went forth, and all the people after him;
18 and they tarried in Beth-merhak. And all his servants
passed on beside him; and all the Cherethites, and all
the Pelethites, and all the Gittites, six hundred men
which came after him from Gath, passed on before the
19 king.   Then said the king to Ittai the Gittite, Wherefore
goest thou also with us? return, and abide with the king:
for thou art a stranger, and also an exile; *return* to thine
20 own place.   Whereas thou camest but yesterday, should
I this day make thee go up and down with us, seeing
I go whither I may? return thou, and take back thy

---

let us flee.   David was taken by surprise.   He left Jerusalem
because (1) Judah and Benjamin were the twofold centre of dis-
affection, and (2) the city was largely inhabited by Jebusites, who
might side with Absalom.

17.   Beth-merhak.   'The Far House,' the last outside the east
gate of Zion before the ford of the Kidron.   Here the king halted,
while his body-guard passed on before him.

18.   the Gittites.   Men of Gath, under the leadership of Ittai,
making with the Cherethites and Pelethites (see note on viii. 18)
a corps of 600 men.

19   thou art a stranger.   David's unselfish thought for his
servants was one secret of his power of winning their fidelity.   In
his early exile his outlaws were always loyal.

brethren; mercy and truth be with thee. And Ittai 21
answered the king, and said, As the LORD liveth, and as
my lord the king liveth, surely in what place my lord the
king shall be, whether for death or for life, even there
also will thy servant be. And David said to Ittai, Go 22
and pass over. And Ittai the Gittite passed over, and all
his men, and all the little ones that were with him. And 23
all the country wept with a loud voice, and all the people
passed over: the king also himself passed over the brook
Kidron, and all the people passed over, toward the way of
the wilderness.

24–29.   *The Ark sent back.*

And, lo, Zadok also *came*, and all the Levites with him, 24
bearing the ark of the covenant of God; and they set
down the ark of God, and Abiathar went up, until all the
people had done passing out of the city. And the king 25
said unto Zadok, Carry back the ark of God into the city:
if I shall find favour in the eyes of the LORD, he will
bring me again, and shew me both it, and his habitation:
but if he say thus, I have no delight in thee; behold, here 26
am I, let him do to me as seemeth good unto him. The 27

---

23.   the way of the wilderness. The wild uninhabited dis-
trict between Jerusalem and the Jordan.

24.   The text is obscure; but the meaning is that Abiathar and
Zadok, the two priests whose duty it was to carry the Ark (*v.* 29),
brought It out, and set It down at the Far House, while the troops
marched past.

the Levites. Probably an addition by the later editor. In
early days the two priests would be enough to perform all that
was done; later, when the services of the Temple became very
elaborate, a large body of Levites was needed to serve the
sanctuary.

25.   It was usual for the king to take the Ark, the Symbol of
Jehovah's Presence, on his expeditions; but in a noble impulse of
faith and resignation David bade the priests bear It back   God
would still be with him; and he was ready to bear any penance
He might impose for his sins.

king said also unto Zadok the priest, Art thou *not* a seer?
return into the city in peace, and your two sons with you,
28 Ahimaaz thy son, and Jonathan the son of Abiathar. See,
I will tarry at the fords of the wilderness, until there come
29 word from you to certify me. Zadok therefore and
Abiathar carried the ark of God again to Jerusalem: and
they abode there.

30-37. *Hushai's Mission to Absalom.*

30   And David went up by the ascent of the *mount of*
Olives, and wept as he went up; and he had his head
covered, and went barefoot: and all the people that were
with him covered every man his head, and they went up,
31 weeping as they went up. And one told David, saying,
Ahithophel is among the conspirators with Absalom.
And David said, O LORD, I pray thee, turn the counsel
32 of Ahithophel into foolishness. And it came to pass, that
when David was come to the top *of the ascent,* where
God was worshipped, behold, Hushai the Archite came
to meet him with his coat rent, and earth upon his head:
33 and David said unto him, If thou passest on with me,
34 then thou shalt be a burden unto me: but if thou return
to the city, and say unto Absalom, I will be thy servant,

---

27. Art thou not a seer? Read, with marg., 'Seest thou?'
Zadok is not elsewhere called a seer, and if he was one there is
no reason for mentioning it here.

30. his head covered &c. Deep grief was expressed by
drawing the headgear closely around the head and face (xix. 4).
Going barefoot was a sign of reverence (Ex. iii. 5), self humiliation
and mourning. Cf. Ezek. xxiv. 17.

31. O Lord, I pray thee. David's prayer was answered at the
moment by the appearance of Hushai.

32. where God was worshipped. High places, existing on
most hills, were commonly used as sanctuaries of Jehovah until the
reforms of Hezekiah. There is no other mention of a shrine on
the Mt of Olives.

34 ff. This scheme is not commended, though according to the
morality of the time it would be justifiable.

O king; as I have been thy father's servant in time past,
so will I now be thy servant: then shalt thou defeat for
me the counsel of Ahithophel. And hast thou not there 35
with thee Zadok and Abiathar the priests? therefore it
shall be, that what thing soever thou shalt hear out of the
king's house, thou shalt tell it to Zadok and Abiathar the
priests. Behold, they have there with them their two 36
sons, Ahimaaz Zadok's son, and Jonathan Abiathar's son;
and by them ye shall send unto me every thing that ye
shall hear. So Hushai David's friend came into the city; 37
and Absalom came into Jerusalem.

xvi. 1-4. *Ziba's Craft.*

And when David was a little past the top *of the ascent,* **16**
behold, Ziba the servant of Mephibosheth met him, with
a couple of asses saddled, and upon them two hundred
loaves of bread, and an hundred clusters of raisins, and
an hundred of summer fruits, and a bottle of wine. And **2**
the king said unto Ziba, What meanest thou by these?
And Ziba said, The asses be for the king's household to
ride on; and the bread and summer fruit for the young
men to eat; and the wine, that such as be faint in the
wilderness may drink. And the king said, And where is **3**
thy master's son? And Ziba said unto the king, Behold,
he abideth at Jerusalem: for he said, To-day shall the
house of Israel restore me the kingdom of my father.
Then said the king to Ziba, Behold, thine is all that **4**
pertaineth unto Mephibosheth. And Ziba said, I do

---

xvi. 1. Ziba. ix. 2 ff.

summer fruits. Probably fresh figs; the season being about
June.

a bottle. A skin, holding a large quantity. A similar present
was brought by Abigail (1 Sam. xxv. 18).

3. for he said. This story is less likely than Mephibosheth's
version in xix. 25 ff.: but David rashly fell into Ziba's trap. He
was a strange mixture of guilelessness and suspicion, patience and
hastiness.

obeisance ; let me find favour in thy sight, my lord, O king.

5-14. *The Curse of Shimei.*

5 And when king David came to Bahurim, behold, there came out thence a man of the family of the house of Saul, whose name was Shimei, the son of Gera : he came out,
6 and cursed still as he came. And he cast stones at David, and at all the servants of king David : and all the people and all the mighty men were on his right hand
7 and on his left. And thus said Shimei when he cursed, Begone, begone, thou man of blood, and man of Belial :
8 the LORD hath returned upon thee all the blood of the house of Saul, in whose stead thou hast reigned ; and the LORD hath delivered the kingdom into the hand of Absalom thy son : and, behold, thou art *taken* in thine
9 own mischief, because thou art a man of blood. Then said Abishai the son of Zeruiah unto the king, Why should this dead dog curse my lord the king ? let me go

---

5. **Shimei.** Of Saul's clan, and naturally hostile to David.

6. **And he cast stones.** The road to Jordan winds down be-tween wild stony hills. On the left stood Shimei; between him and David's men lay a dried torrent bed. Shimei accompanied the march, harassing and insulting David, but out of reach. David refused to allow any of his troops to charge up the hill to end the annoyance.

7 **Begone.** Out of the land, so cleansing the land from his defiling presence—see note on iv. 11. David had 'shed blood abundantly' in his wars, even Israelite blood (iii. 1).

Belial. Worthlessness, i.e. wickedness. It is not a proper name.

8. **the blood of the house of Saul.** Such fierce fanatics as Shimei would not only consider themselves at blood-feud with David, for the deaths of Abner, Ishbosheth and Saul's seven sons (xxi.), but would also misrepresent him as his country's treacherous foe and in part responsible for Saul's defeat and death, since he was the ally of the Philistines in the campaign which led to the disaster of Mt Gilboa, though he took no part in it (1 Sam. xix.).

thine own mischief. He was now betrayed by his son, as he had been false to his father-in-law.

over, I pray thee, and take off his head. And the king 10
said, What have I to do with you, ye sons of Zeruiah?
Because he curseth, and because the LORD hath said
unto him, Curse David; who then shall say, Wherefore
hast thou done so? And David said to Abishai, and to 11
all his servants, Behold, my son, which came forth of my
bowels, seeketh my life: how much more *may* this Benjamite now *do it*? let him alone, and let him curse; for
the LORD hath bidden him. It may be that the LORD 12
will look on the wrong done unto me, and that the LORD
will requite me good for *his* cursing of me this day. So 13
David and his men went by the way: and Shimei went
along on the hill side over against him, and cursed as he
went, and threw stones at him, and cast dust. And the 14
king, and all the people that were with him, came weary;
and he refreshed himself there.

15–19. *Absalom and Hushai.*

And Absalom, and all the people the men of Israel, 15
came to Jerusalem, and Ahithophel with him. And it 16
came to pass, when Hushai the Archite, David's friend,
was come unto Absalom, that Hushai said unto Absalom,
God save the king, God save the king. And Absalom 17

---

10. **What have I** &c.? What have we in common? The
sons of Zeruiah represented the old fierce morality of a passing
heathenism; David, the mercy and justice which a purer faith
in Jehovah was bringing in.

11. **the Lord hath bidden him.** David felt that God was
using Shimei's spite to humiliate and punish him for his sins. So
the prophets taught that the cruelty of the Assyrians was meant
to lead Israel to repentance. Even the supreme crime of the
Crucifixion is spoken of as God's Will (Acts ii. 23).

14. **came weary.** Heb. 'to Ayephim' (as in marg), which
appears to be corrupt. The Lucianic form of the LXX has a
likely reading, 'to the Jordan.'

15. **all the people.** Probably interpolated from *v.* 14.
David's following is described as 'all the people'; Absalom's as
'the men of Israel,' being recruited largely from Judah and
Benjamin.

said to Hushai, Is this thy kindness to thy friend? why
18 wentest thou not with thy friend? And Hushai said unto
Absalom, Nay; but whom the LORD, and this people,
and all the men of Israel have chosen, his will I be, and
19 with him will I abide. And again, whom should I serve?
should I not *serve* in the presence of his son? as I have
served in thy father's presence, so will I be in thy
presence.

20-23. *Ahithophel's Wisdom.*

20 Then said Absalom to Ahithophel, Give your counsel
21 what we shall do. And Ahithophel said unto Absalom,
Go in unto thy father's concubines, which he hath left to
keep the house; and all Israel shall hear that thou art
abhorred of thy father: then shall the hands of all that
22 are with thee be strong. So they spread Absalom a tent
upon the top of the house; and Absalom went in unto
23 his father's concubines in the sight of all Israel. And
the counsel of Ahithophel, which he counselled in those
days, was as if a man inquired at the oracle of God: so
was all the counsel of Ahithophel both with David and
with Absalom.

xvii. 1-4. *Ahithophel's Policy.*

17   Moreover Ahithophel said unto Absalom, Let me now
choose out twelve thousand men, and I will arise and
2 pursue after David this night: and I will come upon him

---

17. thy friend. The 'king's friend' was the title of the
king's confidential adviser. Absalom plays upon the word.

18 f. Hushai was an expert flatterer. Absalom being elected
both by God and the people, what was he to do? After all he
was only transferring his allegiance from father to son.

21. Go in &c. To take possession of the royal harem was
to assume royalty. Cf. iii. 7, xii. 8. Absalom thus proclaimed
himself king. His followers knew that he could not now draw
back and make his peace with David.

xvii. 1. Let me now &c. He hoped by one sudden blow to
paralyse and kill David, so ending all opposition. Fortunately
for David his advice was set aside.

while he is weary and weak handed, and will make him
afraid : and all the people that are with him shall flee ;
and I will smite the king only : and I will bring back all 3
the people unto thee : the man whom thou seekest is as if
all returned : *so* all the people shall be in peace.   And 4
the saying pleased Absalom well, and all the elders of
Israel.

5-14.   *Hushai's Counter-scheme.*

Then said Absalom, Call now Hushai the Archite also, 5
and let us hear likewise what he saith.   And when Hushai 6
was come to Absalom, Absalom spake unto him, saying,
Ahithophel hath spoken after this manner : shall we do
after his saying ? if not, speak thou.   And Hushai said 7
unto Absalom, The counsel that Ahithophel hath given
this time is not good.   Hushai said moreover, Thou 8
knowest thy father and his men, that they be mighty men,
and they be chafed in their minds, as a bear robbed of
her whelps in the field : and thy father is a man of war,
and will not lodge with the people.   Behold, he is hid 9
now in some pit, or in some *other* place : and it will come
to pass, when some of them be fallen at the first, that
whosoever heareth it will say, There is a slaughter among
the people that follow Absalom.   And even he that is 10
valiant, whose heart is as the heart of a lion, shall utterly

---

3.   **and I will** &c.   The LXX gives a better sense : 'And I
will turn all the people to thee, as a bride turns to her husband.
It is only the life of one man thou seekest ; and to all the people
there shall be peace.'   Civil war would be avoided.

4.   **the elders.**   The presence of the sheikhs shews that this
was a full council of war.   Loud approval greeted this cold-
blooded scheme.

7.   **this time.**   Contrasted with his former advice (xvi. 21).

8 ff.   Hushai points out that Ahithophel's plan is not likely to
succeed.   David and his guard, being experienced veterans, would
more probably trap than be trapped by Absalom's untrained
troops.   In that case a panic would certainly put an end to their
hopes.

melt: for all Israel knoweth that thy father is a mighty
11 man, and they which be with him are valiant men. But
I counsel that all Israel be gathered together unto thee,
from Dan even to Beer-sheba, as the sand that is by the
sea for multitude; and that thou go to battle in thine own
12 person. So shall we come upon him in some place where
he shall be found, and we will light upon him as the dew
falleth on the ground: and of him and of all the men that
13 are with him we will not leave so much as one. Moreover,
if he be gotten into a city, then shall all Israel bring
ropes to that city, and we will draw it into the river, until
14 there be not one small stone found there. And Absalom
and all the men of Israel said, The counsel of Hushai the
Archite is better than the counsel of Ahithophel. For
the LORD had ordained to defeat the good counsel of
Ahithophel, to the intent that the LORD might bring evil
upon Absalom.

15-22. *The Message brought to the King.*

15   Then said Hushai unto Zadok and to Abiathar the
priests, Thus and thus did Ahithophel counsel Absalom
and the elders of Israel; and thus and thus have I
16 counselled. Now therefore send quickly, and tell David,
saying, Lodge not this night at the fords of the wilderness,
but in any wise pass over; lest the king be swallowed up,
17 and all the people that are with him. Now Jonathan and
Ahimaaz stayed by En-rogel; and a maidservant used to

---

11 ff. Having raised a wholesome fear of David's resources,
Hushai cleverly plays upon Absalom's vanity by picturing him at
the head of irresistible forces, ensuring victory by a little delay.

14. the Lord had ordained &c. So the disruption of
Rehoboam's kingdom and Ahab's death were ascribed to Divine
Providence (1 Kings xii. 15, xxii. 20).

16. in any wise pass over. So that he would be safe even if
Hushai's advice were rejected.

17. En-rogel. 'The fuller's fountain,' at the S E. corner of
Zion, outside the city. This system of communication was kept
up regularly during Absalom's occupation of Jerusalem.

go and tell them ; and they went and told king David : for they might not be seen to come into the city. But a 18 lad saw them, and told Absalom : and they went both of them away quickly, and came to the house of a man in Bahurim, who had a well in his court ; and they went down thither. And the woman took and spread the 19 covering over the well's mouth, and strewed bruised corn thereon ; and nothing was known. And Absalom's servants 20 came to the woman to the house ; and they said, Where are Ahimaaz and Jonathan? And the woman said unto them, They be gone over the brook of water. And when they had sought and could not find them, they returned to Jerusalem. And it came to pass, after they were 21 departed, that they came up out of the well, and went and told king David ; and they said unto David, Arise ye, and pass quickly over the water : for thus hath Ahithophel counselled against you. Then David arose, and all the 22 people that were with him, and they passed over Jordan : by the morning light there lacked not one of them that was not gone over Jordan.

23. *Ahithophel's Suicide.*

And when Ahithophel saw that his counsel was not 23 followed, he saddled his ass, and arose, and gat him home, unto his city, and set his house in order, and hanged himself ; and he died, and was buried in the sepulchre of his father.

24-26. *Movements of David and Absalom.*

Then David came to Mahanaim. And Absalom passed 24

---

18. they went down. In summer the well, or cistern, was dry.

23. when Ahithophel saw. He knew that the revolt must fail, his revenge against David remain unfulfilled, and he himself put to death as a traitor. This is the first recorded suicide.

24. Mahanaim. In Gilead, the most peaceful and conservative part of Israel ; Ishbosheth's former capital.

25 over Jordan, he and all the men of Israel with him. And
Absalom set Amasa over the host instead of Joab. Now
Amasa was the son of a man, whose name was Ithra the
Israelite, that went in to Abigal the daughter of Nahash,
26 sister to Zeruiah Joab's mother. And Israel and Absalom
pitched in the land of Gilead.

27–29. *Loyalty of Eastern Chiefs.*

27   And it came to pass, when David was come to Mahanaim, that Shobi the son of Nahash of Rabbah of the
children of Ammon, and Machir the son of Ammiel of
28 Lo-debar, and Barzillai the Gileadite of Rogelim, brought
beds, and basons, and earthen vessels, and wheat, and
barley, and meal, and parched *corn*, and beans, and
29 lentils, and parched *pulse*, and honey, and butter, and
sheep, and cheese of kine, for David, and for the people
that were with him, to eat : for they said, The people is
hungry, and weary, and thirsty, in the wilderness.

xviii. 1–8. *The Battle of the Forest of Ephraim.*

18   And David numbered the people that were with him,
and set captains of thousands and captains of hundreds
2 over them. And David sent forth the people, a third
part under the hand of Joab, and a third part under the
hand of Abishai the son of Zeruiah, Joab's brother, and a
third part under the hand of Ittai the Gittite. And the
king said unto the people, I will surely go forth with you

Absalom passed over Jordan. He had had time to collect a
large army.

25. Ithra the Israelite. Read (marg.), 'Jether the Ishmaelite,'
as in 1 Chr. ii. 17. He married David's half-sister (daughter
of Nahash, not Jesse), so that his son Amasa was cousin to
Absalom and Joab.

27. Shobi. Brother of Hanun, David's enemy (x. 1 ff.);
now probably governor of Rabbah.

Machir. Formerly Mephibosheth's guardian (ix. 4).

myself also. But the people said, Thou shalt not go 3
forth: for if we flee away, they will not care for us;
neither if half of us die, will they care for us: but thou
art worth ten thousand of us: therefore now it is better
that thou be ready to succour us out of the city. And 4
the king said unto them, What seemeth you best I will
do. And the king stood by the gate side, and all the
people went out by hundreds and by thousands. And 5
the king commanded Joab and Abishai and Ittai, saying,
Deal gently for my sake with the young man, even with
Absalom. And all the people heard when the king gave
all the captains charge concerning Absalom. So the 6
people went out into the field against Israel: and the
battle was in the forest of Ephraim. And the people of 7
Israel were smitten there before the servants of David,
and there was a great slaughter there that day of twenty
thousand men. For the battle was there spread over the 8
face of all the country: and the forest devoured more
people that day than the sword devoured.

9–18.   *Absalom's Death.*

And Absalom chanced to meet the servants of David. 9
And Absalom rode upon his mule, and the mule went
under the thick boughs of a great oak, and his head
caught hold of the oak, and he was taken up between the

---

xviii. 3. Thou shalt not go forth. David had narrowly
escaped death in a battle with the Philistines, since when his
troops discouraged his fighting in person (xxi. 17).

6.   the forest of Ephraim. A jungle in Gilead.

8.   the forest devoured &c. Possibly the ground was broken
with rocky clefts covered with brushwood, into which the fleeing
troops fell and were killed.

9.   In his flight Absalom rode into a party of David's men.
He turned his mule (the royal beast) in the direction of some
well-known oak or terebinth. As he was carried beneath this
and perhaps turning to see his pursuers, his head was apparently
caught in a fork of the tree and held helpless. There is nothing
to shew that he was caught by his long hair.

heaven and the earth ; and the mule that was under him
10 went on.   And a certain man saw it, and told Joab, and
11 said, Behold, I saw Absalom hanging in an oak.   And
Joab said unto the man that told him, And, behold, thou
sawest it, and why didst thou not smite him there to the
ground ? and I would have given thee ten *pieces of* silver,
12 and a girdle.   And the man said unto Joab, Though I
should receive a thousand *pieces of* silver in mine hand,
yet would I not put forth mine hand against the king's
son : for in our hearing the king charged thee and
Abishai and Ittai, saying, Beware that none touch the
13 young man Absalom.   Otherwise if I had dealt falsely
against his life, (and there is no matter hid from the king,)
14 then thou thyself wouldest have stood aloof.   Then said
Joab, I may not tarry thus with thee.   And he took three
darts in his hand, and thrust them through the heart of
Absalom, while he was yet alive in the midst of the oak.
15 And ten young men that bare Joab's armour compassed
16 about and smote Absalom, and slew him.   And Joab blew
the trumpet, and the people returned from pursuing after
17 Israel : for Joab held back the people.   And they took
Absalom, and cast him into the great pit in the forest,
and raised over him a very great heap of stones : and all
18 Israel fled every one to his tent.   Now Absalom in his

---

13.   if I had dealt &c.   The man states that if he had slain
Absalom and been charged for it before the king, Joab would
not have protected him.

14.   By slaying Absalom Joab was inflicting a well-deserved
punishment, putting an end to the civil war, paying off his own
score for the firing of his field (xiv. 30), and disobeying David's
express orders.

16.   Joab blew the trumpet.   The head of the revolt being
dead, there was no need for further slaughter.

17.   heap of stones.   As over Achan and the king of Ai,
both foes of Israel (Josh. vii. 26, viii. 29).

tent.   An antiquated expression for 'home,' a survival from
the nomadic stage of society.   Cf. **xx. 22.**

life time had taken and reared up for himself the pillar, which is in the king's dale : for he said, I have no son to keep my name in remembrance : and he called the pillar after his own name : and it is called Absalom's monument, unto this day.

19–23. *The two Runners.*

Then said Ahimaaz the son of Zadok, Let me now run, 19 and bear the king tidings, how that the LORD hath avenged him of his enemies.   And Joab said unto him, 20 Thou shalt not be the bearer of tidings this day, but thou shalt bear tidings another day : but this day thou shalt bear no tidings, because the king's son is dead.   Then 21 said Joab to the Cushite, Go tell the king what thou hast seen.   And the Cushite bowed himself unto Joab, and ran.   Then said Ahimaaz the son of Zadok yet again to 22 Joab, But come what may, let me, I pray thee, also run after the Cushite.   And Joab said, Wherefore wilt thou run, my son, seeing that thou wilt have no reward for the tidings ?   But come what may, *said he*, I will run.   And 23 he said unto him, Run.   Then Ahimaaz ran by the way of the Plain, and overran the Cushite.

---

18. the king's dale. The site is unknown. Cp. Gen. xiv. 17.

I have no son. In xiv. 27, he is said to have three sons. These may have died in infancy. This account is the earlier and more trustworthy of the two.

20. Joab was unwilling to expose so important a person as Ahimaaz to the danger of bearing evil news to David. Cf. iv. 10.

21. the Cushite. Either an Ethiopian or an Arabian. His death would not matter.

22. come what may. Ahimaaz is willing to take the risk.

23. the way of the Plain. By the Jordan Valley and up the highway to Mahanaim, the longer but quicker way. Cf. ii. 29. The straight route, taken by the Cushite, was probably across broken country.

24-33. The Tidings brought to David.

24 Now David sat between the two gates : and the watchman went up to the roof of the gate unto the wall, and
lifted up his eyes, and looked, and, behold, a man running
25 alone.   And the watchman cried, and told the king.
And the king said, If he be alone, there is tidings in his
26 mouth.   And he came apace, and drew near.   And the
watchman saw another man running : and the watchman
called unto the porter, and said, Behold, *another* man
running alone.   And the king said, He also bringeth
27 tidings.   And the watchman said, Me thinketh the running
of the foremost is like the running of Ahimaaz the son of
Zadok.   And the king said, He is a good man, and
28 cometh with good tidings.   And Ahimaaz called, and said
unto the king, All is well.   And he bowed himself before
the king with his face to the earth, and said, Blessed be
the LORD thy God, which hath delivered up the men that
29 lifted up their hand against my lord the king.   And the
king said, Is it well with the young man Absalom ?   And
Ahimaaz answered, When Joab sent the king's servant,
even me thy servant, I saw a great tumult, but I knew
30 not what it was.   And the king said, Turn aside, and
31 stand here.   And he turned aside, and stood still.   And,
behold, the Cushite came ; and the Cushite said, Tidings
for my lord the king : for the LORD hath avenged thee
32 this day of all them that rose up against thee.   And the
king said unto the Cushite, Is it well with the young man

---

24.   between the two gates.   The space between the outer
and inner gates.   Cf. note on xv. 2.

25.   If he be alone.   Fugitives flying from defeat would
come in numbers, not singly.

27.   He is a good man &c.   David knew that Joab would
not send evil news by so important a person.   Cf. note on *v.* 20.

28.   All is well.   Read, ' Peace ' (marg.).   His courage fails,
he greets the king, and falls on his face.

Absalom? And the Cushite answered, The enemies of
my lord the king, and all that rise up against thee to do
thee hurt, be as that young man is. And the king was 33
much moved, and went up to the chamber over the gate,
and wept: and as he went, thus he said, O my son
Absalom, my son, my son Absalom! would God I had
died for thee, O Absalom, my son, my son!

xix. 1–8a. *Joab's Rebuke.*

And it was told Joab, Behold, the king weepeth and **19**
mourneth for Absalom. And the victory that day was 2
turned into mourning unto all the people: for the people
heard say that day, The king grieveth for his son. And 3
the people gat them by stealth that day into the city, as
people that are ashamed steal away when they flee in
battle. And the king covered his face, and the king 4
cried with a loud voice, O my son Absalom, O Absalom,
my son, my son! And Joab came into the house to the 5
king, and said, Thou hast shamed this day the faces of
all thy servants, which this day have saved thy life, and
the lives of thy sons and of thy daughters, and the lives
of thy wives, and the lives of thy concubines; in that 6
thou lovest them that hate thee, and hatest them that
love thee. For thou hast declared this day, that princes

---

32. The enemies &c. This tactful message was probably
dictated verbally by Joab.

33. the king was much moved. Not only by natural grief,
but by the more bitter sorrow for his own weakness and sin,
through which he had brought so much disaster upon himself
and upon Israel.

xix. 2. The king's grief so powerfully affected the feeling of the
troops, that they slunk home as though they had been defeated.
He had always an extraordinary power of winning devotion.
Cf. iii. 36, and note on xv. 19.

5 ff. Joab accused David of forgetting in his private grief the
gratitude he owed to the loyalty of those who had saved his life
and throne, and warned him of the danger of a sudden revulsion
of feeling.

and servants are nought unto thee : for this day I perceive,
that if Absalom had lived, and all we had died this day,
7 then it had pleased thee well. Now therefore arise, go
forth, and speak comfortably unto thy servants : for I
swear by the LORD, if thou go not forth, there will not
tarry a man with thee this night : and that will be worse
unto thee than all the evil that hath befallen thee from
8 thy youth until now. Then the king arose, and sat in the
gate. And they told unto all the people, saying, Behold,
the king doth sit in the gate : and all the people came
before the king.

8*b*-10. *The Perplexity of Israel.*

9 Now Israel had fled every man to his tent. And all the
people were at strife throughout all the tribes of Israel,
saying, The king delivered us out of the hand of our
enemies, and he saved us out of the hand of the Philistines ; and now he is fled out of the land from Absalom.
10 And Absalom, whom we anointed over us, is dead in
battle. Now therefore why speak ye not a word of bringing the king back ?

11-15. *David's secret Overtures to Judah.*

11   And king David sent to Zadok and Abiathar the priests,
saying, Speak unto the elders of Judah, saying, Why are
ye the last to bring the king back to his house ? seeing

---

8. Israel. Those who had followed Absalom.

9. all the people. The rebellion had been mainly the work
of the chiefs. The people, sobered by the present distress and
the thought of David's past glories, expostulated with their
leaders for their slowness in restoring David.

11. Why are ye the last &c. Judah's disloyalty was the
result of David's attempt to weld together North and South into
one kingdom. The balance of power had necessarily gone to
the North. (Cf. note on xv. 9.) David now attempted to bind
Judah more closely to his interest. He made a strong appeal
to the sentiment of kinship (*v.* 12). But in addition he practically
put himself into the hands of the Judaean chiefs by appointing
Amasa, the late leader of the rebels, to supersede Joab, whom

the speech of all Israel is come to the king, *to bring him*
to his house.   Ye are my brethren, ye are my bone and 12
my flesh : wherefore then are ye the last to bring back
the king ?   And say ye to Amasa, Art thou not my bone 13
and my flesh ?   God do so to me, and more also, if thou
be not captain of the host before me continually in the
room of Joab.   And he bowed the heart of all the men of 14
Judah, even as *the heart of* one man ; so that they sent
unto the king, *saying*, Return thou, and all thy servants.
So the king returned, and came to Jordan.   And Judah 15
came to Gilgal, to go to meet the king, to bring the king
over Jordan.

16–23.   *Shimei's Penitence.*

And Shimei the son of Gera, the Benjamite, which was 16
of Bahurim, hasted and came down with the men of
Judah to meet king David.   And there were a thousand 17
men of Benjamin with him, and Ziba the servant of the
house of Saul, and his fifteen sons and his twenty servants
with him ; and they went through Jordan in the presence
of the king.   And there went over a ferry boat to bring 18
over the king's household, and to do what he thought
good.   And Shimei the son of Gera fell down before the
king, when he was come over Jordan.   And he said unto 19
the king, Let not my lord impute iniquity unto me, neither
do thou remember that which thy servant did perversely
the day that my lord the king went out of Jerusalem, that
the king should take it to his heart.   For thy servant 20
doth know that I have sinned : therefore, behold, I am

---

he could not forgive for Absalom's death (*v.* 13).   Thus David
committed himself more definitely to the South, with the result
that a new rebellion broke out in the North (**xx.**).

16.   The result of the negotiations was seen in the friendly
meeting of David with the men of Benjamin (under Shimei and
Ziba) and Judah at the fords of the Jordan.   The northern
tribes were not bidden, perhaps because David did not regard
them as dangerous.

come this day the first of all the house of Joseph to go
21 down to meet my lord the king.   But Abishai the son of
Zeruiah answered and said, Shall not Shimei be put to
death for this, because he cursed the LORD's anointed?
22 And David said, What have I to do with you, ye sons of
Zeruiah, that ye should this day be adversaries unto me?
shall there any man be put to death this day in Israel?
for do not I know that I am this day king over Israel?
23 And the king said unto Shimei, Thou shalt not die.   And
the king sware unto him.

24–30. *Mephibosheth's Case.*

24   And Mephibosheth the son of Saul came down to meet
the king; and he had neither dressed his feet, nor trimmed
his beard, nor washed his clothes, from the day the king
25 departed until the day he came home in peace.   And it
came to pass, when he was come to Jerusalem to meet
the king, that the king said unto him, Wherefore wentest
26 not thou with me, Mephibosheth?   And he answered, My
lord, O king, my servant deceived me: for thy servant
said, I will saddle me an ass, that I may ride thereon,
27 and go with the king; because thy servant is lame.   And
he hath slandered thy servant unto my lord the king; but
my lord the king is as an angel of God: do therefore
28 what is good in thine eyes.   For all my father's house
were but dead men before my lord the king: yet didst

---

22. adversaries.   A passionate rebuke (Hebrew, 'Satans').
See note on xxiv. 1.
24. came down.   To Jerusalem from his place in the
highlands of Benjamin, where he had fled during Absalom's
occupation of Jerusalem.   Chronologically this meeting follows
xx. 3.

he had neither &c.   He had lived as a mourner.
26. my servant deceived me.   He had ordered Ziba to
saddle the ass that he might ride with David.   Ziba had used
the asses for his own ends and had given a slanderous account
of his master (xvi. 1 ff.).
27. as an angel.   Infallible in judgment.   Cf. xiv. 17–20.

thou set thy servant among them that did eat at thine
own table. What right therefore have I yet that I should
cry any more unto the king? And the king said unto 29
him, Why speakest thou any more of thy matters? I
say, Thou and Ziba divide the land. And Mephibosheth 30
said unto the king, Yea, let him take all, forasmuch as my
lord the king is come in peace unto his own house.

31-39. *Barzillai's Farewell.*

And Barzillai the Gileadite came down from Rogelim ; 31
and he went over Jordan with the king, to conduct him
over Jordan. Now Barzillai was a very aged man, even 32
fourscore years old : and he had provided the king with
sustenance while he lay at Mahanaim ; for he was a very
great man. And the king said unto Barzillai, Come thou 33
over with me, and I will sustain thee with me in Jerusalem.
And Barzillai said unto the king, How many are the days 34
of the years of my life, that I should go up with the king
unto Jerusalem? I am this day fourscore years old : can 35
I discern between good and bad? can thy servant taste
what I eat or what I drink? can I hear any more the
voice of singing men and singing women? wherefore then
should thy servant be yet a burden unto my lord the
king? Thy servant would but just go over Jordan with 36
the king : and why should the king recompense it me
with such a reward? Let thy servant, I pray thee, turn 37
back again, that I may die in mine own city, by the grave
of my father and my mother. But behold, thy servant
Chimham ; let him go over with my lord the king ; and

---

29. Thou and Ziba &c. Another hasty decision. Ziba was
a powerful Benjamite chief, and David was anxious to conciliate
Benjamin. The compromise probably satisfied neither party.

30. Yea, let him take all. Merely Oriental etiquette.

31. Barzillai. A chief of the old school, holding to the
simple country ways of his fathers, with no taste for the splendour
and luxury of city life now growing up at Jerusalem (*v.* 35).

37. Chimham. Barzillai's son (1 Kings ii. 7).

38 do to him what shall seem good unto thee. And the king
answered, Chimham shall go over with me, and I will do
to him that which shall seem good unto thee : and whatsoever thou shalt require of me, that will I do for thee.
39 And all the people went over Jordan, and the king went
over : and the king kissed Barzillai, and blessed him;
and he returned unto his own place.

40-43.   *Hot Words between North and South.*

40   So the king went over to Gilgal, and Chimham went
over with him: and all the people of Judah brought the
41 king over, and also half the people of Israel. And,
behold, all the men of Israel came to the king, and said
unto the king, Why have our brethren the men of Judah
stolen thee away, and brought the king, and his house-
42 hold, over Jordan, and all David's men with him? And
all the men of Judah answered the men of Israel, Because
the king is near of kin to us: wherefore then be ye angry
for this matter? have we eaten at all of the king's cost?
43 or hath he given us any gift? And the men of Israel
answered the men of Judah, and said, We have ten parts
in the king, and we have also more *right* in David than
ye: why then did ye despise us, that our advice should

---

41. all the men of Israel. The amity of the meeting at
Gilgal is broken in upon by an embassy from the northern
tribes, whose hesitation (*vv.* 9 f.) was now at an end. Their
complaint is that they had not been invited to this conference,
though they formed the chief part of the kingdom, and had
been first to suggest that overtures should be made to the king
(*v.* 43 marg.).

42. The Judaeans maintain that they took precedence, as the
king's tribe, yet that their position had conferred no privilege
upon them.

43. we have also &c. The LXX gives better sense, 'I am
also the firstborn rather than thou.' Reuben was Jacob's eldest
son.

that our advice. Read (marg.), 'were not we the first to
speak of bringing back our king?'

not be first had in bringing back our king? And the
words of the men of Judah were fiercer than the words of
the men of Israel.

(*e*) **xx.** *The Revolt of Sheba.*

1-3. *The Revolt begins. David returns to Jerusalem.*

And there happened to be there a man of Belial, whose **20**
name was Sheba, the son of Bichri, a Benjamite: and he
blew the trumpet, and said, We have no portion in David,
neither have we inheritance in the son of Jesse: every
man to his tents, O Israel. So all the men of Israel went **2**
up from following David, and followed Sheba the son of
Bichri: but the men of Judah clave unto their king, from
Jordan even to Jerusalem.

And David came to his house at Jerusalem; and the **3**
king took the ten women his concubines, whom he had
left to keep the house, and put them in ward, and provided them with sustenance, but went not in unto them.
So they were shut up unto the day of their death, living in
widowhood.

4-13. *The Murder of Amasa.*

Then said the king to Amasa, Call me the men of Judah **4**
together within three days, and be thou here present. So **5**
Amasa went to call *the men of* Judah together: but he
tarried longer than the set time which he had appointed
him. And David said to Abishai, Now shall Sheba the **6**

---

xx. 1. Belial. See xvi. 7 note.

We have no portion. The same war-cry was raised in
Jeroboam's rising against the Davidic Dynasty (1 Kings xii.
16). It implies a return to the old tribal independence. This
revolt arose out of David's concessions to Judah (xix. 11 ff.).

4. Amasa. Now commander-in-chief in Joab's place (xix. 13).

5. he tarried. He failed partly through lack of ability,
partly it may be through lack of will. The Judaean chiefs may
not have been eager to keep up the unity of the kingdom.
Judah was more important, when David was king of Judah only.

6. Abishai. David could scarcely ask Joab, whom he had
just deposed.

son of Bichri do us more harm than did Absalom: take thou thy lord's servants, and pursue after him, lest he get

7 him fenced cities, and escape out of our sight. And there went out after him Joab's men, and the Cherethites and the Pelethites, and all the mighty men: and they went out of Jerusalem, to pursue after Sheba the son of Bichri.

8 When they were at the great stone which is in Gibeon, Amasa came to meet them. And Joab was girded with his apparel of war that he had put on, and thereon was a girdle with a sword fastened upon his loins in the sheath

9 thereof; and as he went forth it fell out. And Joab said to Amasa, Is it well with thee, my brother? And Joab took Amasa by the beard with his right hand to kiss him.

10 But Amasa took no heed to the sword that was in Joab's hand: so he smote him therewith in the belly, and shed out his bowels to the ground, and struck him not again; and he died. And Joab and Abishai his brother pursued

11 after Sheba the son of Bichri. And there stood by him one of Joab's young men, and said, He that favoureth

12 Joab, and he that is for David, let him follow Joab. And Amasa lay wallowing in his blood in the midst of the high way. And when the man saw that all the people stood still, he carried Amasa out of the high way into the field, and cast a garment over him, when he saw that every one

13 that came by him stood still. When he was removed out of the high way, all the people went on after Joab, to pursue after Sheba the son of Bichri.

---

7. Joab's men. Some read, 'Joab.' For the time he marched under his brother's command; but he was waiting his opportunity.

10. the sword that was in Joab's hand. Perhaps a dagger concealed in his left hand. He had purposely dropped his sword in order to allay Amasa's suspicions.

11. he that is for David. Implies that Amasa was not loyal to David.

14-22. *The End of Sheba.*

And he went through all the tribes of Israel unto Abel, 14
and to Beth-maacah, and all the Berites: and they were
gathered together, and went also after him. And they 15
came and besieged him in Abel of Beth-maacah, and
they cast up a mount against the city, and it stood against
the rampart: and all the people that were with Joab
battered the wall, to throw it down. Then cried a wise 16
woman out of the city, Hear, hear; say, I pray you, unto
Joab, Come near hither, that I may speak with thee.
And he came near unto her; and the woman said, Art 17
thou Joab? And he answered, I am. Then she said
unto him, Hear the words of thine handmaid. And he
answered, I do hear. Then she spake, saying, They 18
were wont to speak in old time, saying, They shall surely
ask *counsel* at Abel: and so they ended *the matter*.
I am of them that are peaceable and faithful in Israel: 19
thou seekest to destroy a city and a mother in Israel: why

---

14. And he went. i.e. Sheba. His march was an attempt
to rouse the Israelites, which failed. He was 'a man of Belial'
(note on xvi. 7), not a man of influence. Only his own clansmen,
the Bichrites, rose ('Berites' is probably a scribe's error). He
reached Abel, in the far north, where he attempted to make a
stand.

15. a mount. A mound was built against the outer wall;
standing on which they battered the upper and weaker part of
the ramparts.

16. a wise woman. See note on xiv. 2.

18. They shall surely &c. People (she claims) were wont
to ask counsel of Abel, as of an oracle. The LXX however gives
better sense : ' They were wont to quote a proverb in old time,
saying, Ask in Abel and Dan whether anything has ever fallen
into disuse which the faithful of Israel had once ordained.'
Abel was one of the two towns where Hebrew customs
were faithfully preserved. In an age of unlimited veneration
for custom, this was the highest praise. Joab might well
hesitate to destroy a town of so fair fame.

19. a mother in Israel. A city venerable in age, and
important by reason of her daughter villages (cf. Ezek. xvi. 46).

20 wilt thou swallow up the inheritance of the LORD? And
   Joab answered and said, Far be it, far be it from me, that
21 I should swallow up or destroy. The matter is not so:
   but a man of the hill country of Ephraim, Sheba the son
   of Bichri by name, hath lifted up his hand against the
   king, even against David: deliver him only, and I will
   depart from the city. And the woman said unto Joab,
   Behold, his head shall be thrown to thee over the wall.
22 Then the woman went unto all the people in her wisdom.
   And they cut off the head of Sheba the son of Bichri, and
   threw it out to Joab. And he blew the trumpet, and they
   were dispersed from the city, every man to his tent. And
   Joab returned to Jerusalem unto the king.

23-26. *A List of Officials.*

23 Now Joab was over all the host of Israel: and Benaiah
   the son of Jehoiada was over the Cherethites and over the
24 Pelethites· and Adoram was over the tribute: and
25 Jehoshaphat the son of Ahilud was the recorder: and
   Sheva was scribe: and Zadok and Abiathar were priests:
26 and Ira also the Jairite was priest unto David.

D. THE APPENDIX. XXI.–XXIV.

The Court Record (ix.–xx.) is continued in 1 Kings i. and ii.
This section, which breaks into it, contained originally two
accounts of Divine visitation (xxi. 1–14, xxiv.), both of which
occurred early in David's reign. A later editor placed between
these some records of David's heroes (xxi. 15–22, xxiii. 8–39).
A third editor inserted into the midst of these records two songs
of David (xxii , xxiii. 1–7).

---

20. Far be it. At the battles of Gibeon and Ephraim Joab
had shewn his unwillingness to shed blood unnecessarily.

22. the woman went unto all the people &c. The LXX is
again clearer : 'went into the city and spoke unto all the people
in her wisdom.'

24. the tribute. The levy (marg.), i.e. gangs of forced
labourers ; an institution especially hateful to the independent
Israelites. Through it Rehoboam lost half his kingdom and
Adoram his life (1 Kings xii. 4, 18).

xxi. 1–14. *The Famine.*

This, and the account in xxiv , are probably extracts from a collection of judicial records preserved perhaps in the Temple. Custom and precedent, especially where a clear manifestation of Jehovah's will could be quoted, formed the basis of Hebrew legislation. Underneath the primitive ideas embodied in this expiation of Saul's guilt there lie these moral principles : that promises must be kept ; that God punishes men's breach of faith to each other ; that national and family life is continuous, and the consequences of our actions do not come to an end with ourselves.

And there was a famine in the days of David three **21** years, year after year; and David sought the face of the LORD. And the LORD said, It is for Saul, and for his bloody house, because he put to death the Gibeonites. And the king called the Gibeonites, and said unto them ; **2** (now the Gibeonites were not of the children of Israel, but of the remnant of the Amorites ; and the children of Israel had sworn unto them : and Saul sought to slay them in his zeal for the children of Israel and Judah :) and David said unto the Gibeonites, What shall I do for **3** you? and wherewith shall I make atonement, that ye may bless the inheritance of the LORD? And the Gibeonites **4** said unto him, It is no matter of silver or gold between us

---

xxi. 1. famine. Want of corn, the result of insufficient winter rain, for three years running. This probably happened in the early years of David at Jerusalem.

sought the face of the Lord. Probably by Urim and Thummim. See note on ii. 1.

his bloody house. By breaking Israel's covenant with Gibeon (see Josh. ix.) Saul had defiled the land (note on iv. 11), which therefore God would not fertilize.

2. Amorites. Canaanite highlanders of Benjamin, Dan and Judah.

3. the inheritance of the Lord. The land of Israel. See note on xiv. 16.

4. It is no matter &c. The difficulties are, (1) Saul's guilt is too serious to admit of money compensation (this was afterwards forbidden, see Numb. xxxv. 31), and (2) the Gibeonites being outlanders had no legal right of blood-revenge against

and Saul, or his house; neither is it for us to put any man
to death in Israel. And he said, What ye shall say, that
5 will I do for you. And they said unto the king, The man
that consumed us, and that devised against us, *that* we
should be destroyed from remaining in any of the borders
6 of Israel, let seven men of his sons be delivered unto us,
and we will hang them up unto the LORD in Gibeah of
Saul, the chosen of the LORD. And the king said, I will
7 give them. But the king spared Mephibosheth, the son
of Jonathan the son of Saul, because of the LORD'S oath
that was between them, between David and Jonathan the
8 son of Saul. But the king took the two sons of Rizpah
the daughter of Aiah, whom she bare unto Saul, Armoni
and Mephibosheth; and the five sons of Michal the
daughter of Saul, whom she bare to Adriel the son of
9 Barzillai the Meholathite: and he delivered them into the
hands of the Gibeonites, and they hanged them in the
mountain before the LORD, and they fell *all* seven together: and they were put to death in the days of harvest,
10 in the first days, at the beginning of barley harvest. And
Rizpah the daughter of Aiah took sackcloth, and spread
it for her upon the rock, from the beginning of harvest
until water was poured upon them from heaven; and she

---

an Israelite house. It is a case without precedent to be decided
by the king's supreme prerogative. Accordingly David invites
them to state their claim.

6. seven. A sacred number, often used in sacrifice. Cf.
Numb. xxiii. 1.

Gibeah. LXX has Gibeon, the scene of the crime.

8. Rizpah. See iii. 7.

Michal. A mistake. Merab, not Michal, was Adriel's wife
(1 Sam. xviii. 19).

10. from the beginning &c. i.e. from April to October, a
watch of six months. Her object was to ensure their ultimate
burial, without which they would be unable to rest in Sheol.
(Introd. p. xiv.)

until water was poured. The sign that Jehovah had accepted
the sacrifice. To expose the bodies longer was unnecessary.

suffered neither the birds of the air to rest on them by
day, nor the beasts of the field by night.   And it was told 11
David what Rizpah the daughter of Aiah, the concubine
of Saul, had done.   And David went and took the bones 12
of Saul and the bones of Jonathan his son from the men
of Jabesh-gilead, which had stolen them from the street of
Beth-shan, where the Philistines had hanged them, in the
day that the Philistines slew Saul in Gilboa: and he 13
brought up from thence the bones of Saul and the bones
of Jonathan his son; and they gathered the bones of them
that were hanged.   And they buried the bones of Saul 14
and Jonathan his son in the country of Benjamin in Zela,
in the sepulchre of Kish his father: and they performed
all that the king commanded.   And after that God was
intreated for the land.

15–22.   *Exploits in the Philistine Wars.*

And the Philistines had war again with Israel; and 15
David went down, and his servants with him, and fought
against the Philistines: and David waxed faint.   And 16
Ishbi-benob, which was of the sons of the giant, the
weight of whose spear was three hundred *shekels* of brass
in weight, he being girded with a new *sword*, thought
to have slain David.   But Abishai the son of Zeruiah 17
succoured him, and smote the Philistine, and killed him.
Then the men of David sware unto him, saying, Thou
shalt go no more out with us to battle, that thou quench
not the lamp of Israel.

---

12. And David went.   That David harboured no malicious
resentment against Saul's house is clear (cf. esp. i. 17–27); yet
he did not escape the hatred of the Benjamites (see note on
xvi. 8).

15. the Philistines.   These wars probably filled some years
after David's capture of Jerusalem.   We have a very meagre
account of them in ch. v. and viii. 1.

went down.   From the highlands of Judah to the lower
Philistine country.

18   And it came to pass after this, that there was again war
with the Philistines at Gob: then Sibbecai the Hushathite
19 slew Saph, which was of the sons of the giant. And there
was again war with the Philistines at Gob; and Elhanan
the son of Jaare-oregim the Beth-lehemite slew Goliath
the Gittite, the staff of whose spear was like a weaver's
20 beam. And there was again war at Gath, where was a
man of great stature, that had on every hand six fingers,
and on every foot six toes, four and twenty in number;
21 and he also was born to the giant. And when he defied
Israel, Jonathan the son of Shimei David's brother slew
22 him. These four were born to the giant in Gath; and
they fell by the hand of David, and by the hand of his
servants.

xxii. (= Pṣ. xviii.). *David's Triumph Song.*

This hymn celebrates past victories and the prospect of
security from without and settled government within. No
shadow of sin and disaster has as yet fallen. It therefore
belongs to the earlier years of David's reign. Some of the
thoughts and expressions seem to belong to a later age, and may
be due to later editing; but the main ideas are most appropriate
to David's own experience.

22   And David spake unto the LORD the words of this song
in the day that the LORD delivered him out of the hand
2   of all his enemies, and out of the hand of Saul: and he
said,

---

19. Elhanan the son of Jaare-oregim. Oregim = 'weavers,'
and may have slipped in from the next line. He is called 'the
son of Jair' in 1 Chron. xx. 5.
Goliath the Gittite. The name of David's foe (1 Sam. xvii.).
Either there were two Goliaths of Gath, or the name of the
more famous giant was given to David's foe by later tradition.
xxii. 1. the Lord delivered him. David traced Divine
Providence especially in his marvellous escapes from Saul's
persecution (1 Sam. xxiii. 14 &c.) and his victories over the
Philistines (v. 17-25).

(*a*) *The Ascription.* 2-4.

The LORD is my rock, and my fortress, and my
    deliverer, even mine;
The God of my rock, in him will I trust;   3
My shield, and the horn of my salvation, my high
    tower, and my refuge;
My saviour, thou savest me from violence.
I will call upon the LORD, who is worthy to be 4
    praised:
So shall I be saved from mine enemies.

(*b*) *David's Prayer in Peril.* 5-7.

For the waves of death compassed me,   5
The floods of ungodliness made me afraid.
The cords of Sheol were round about me: 6
The snares of death came upon me.
In my distress I called upon the LORD,   7
Yea, I called unto my God:
And he heard my voice out of his temple,
And my cry *came* into his ears.

(*c*) *God's Appearing.* 8-16.

Then the earth shook and trembled,   8
The foundations of heaven moved
And were shaken, because he was wroth.

---

2. my rock. David's early warfare had been mostly waged
from mountain strongholds and hiding places.

5, 6. David had complained 'there is but a step between me
and death' (1 Sam. xx. 3), when Saul tried to catch him. He
had also had narrow escapes in the Philistine wars (xxi. 16).

Sheol. See note on xii. 23.

8. The foundations of heaven. Mountains, which seem like
pillars supporting the sky.

he was wroth. This great storm and earthquake were a sign
that Jehovah was moved with anger against His and Israel's
enemies.

9   There went up a smoke out of his nostrils,
    And fire out of his mouth devoured:
    Coals were kindled by it.

10 He bowed the heavens also, and came down;
    And thick darkness was under his feet.

11 And he rode upon a cherub, and did fly:
    Yea, he was seen upon the wings of the wind.

12 And he made darkness pavilions round about him,
    Gathering of waters, thick clouds of the skies.

13 At the brightness before him
    Coals of fire were kindled.

14 The LORD thundered from heaven,
    And the Most High uttered his voice.

15 And he sent out arrows, and scattered them;
    Lightning, and discomfited them.

16 Then the channels of the sea appeared,
    The foundations of the world were laid bare,
    By the rebuke of the LORD,
    At the blast of the breath of his nostrils.

(d) *God's Deliverance.*   17-20.

17 He sent from on high, he took me;
    He drew me out of many waters;

18 He delivered me from my strong enemy,
    From them that hated me; for they were too mighty
        for me.

---

9 ff.   Remembering how Jehovah revealed Himself at the Red Sea and Mount Sinai by such disturbances of nature, David recognised His presence and guidance in the storm that gathered over the Philistines at Baal-perazim and in the Valley of Rephaim (v. 17 ff.).

17.   As He drew Moses out of the Nile, and His people from the Red Sea, so He had drawn Israel out of the overwhelming distresses of Philistine oppression.

18. too mighty for me.   Israel seemed no match for Philistia.

They came upon me in the day of my calamity: 19
But the LORD was my stay.
He brought me forth also into a large place: 20
He delivered me, because he delighted in me.

(e) God's Delight in Goodness and Mercy. 21–31.

The LORD rewarded me according to my righteous- 21
    ness:
According to the cleanness of my hands hath he re-
    compensed me.
For I have kept the ways of the LORD,   22
And have not wickedly departed from my God.
For all his judgements were before me: 23
And as for his statutes, I did not depart from them.
I was also perfect toward him,   24
And I kept myself from mine iniquity.
Therefore hath the LORD recompensed me according 25
    to my righteousness;
According to my cleanness in his eyesight.
With the merciful thou wilt shew thyself merciful,   26
With the perfect man thou wilt shew thyself perfect;
With the pure thou wilt shew thyself pure;   27
And with the perverse thou wilt shew thyself froward.
And the afflicted people thou wilt save: 28
But thine eyes are upon the haughty, that thou mayest
    bring them down.

---

20. a large place. Freedom and enlarged borders.

21 ff. God rejected Saul for his self-will and violence. David
was 'the man after God's own heart,' whose law was God's
will, and whose pattern was God's goodness. Obviously this
was before David's great sin.

26. With the merciful. David had been merciful to Saul
and his house (1 Sam. xxiv.; 2 Sam. iii. 1, ix. 1 ff.) and God
had been merciful to him.

28. the afflicted. David under Saul, and Israel under the
Philistines.

the haughty. Philistia was considered so. See i. 20.

29 For thou art my lamp, O LORD:
    And the LORD will lighten my darkness.
30 For by thee I run upon a troop:
    By my God do I leap over a wall.
31 As for God, his way is perfect:
    The word of the LORD is tried;
    He is a shield unto all them that trust in him.

(*f*) *Victory ascribed to Jehovah.* 32-37.

32 For who is God, save the LORD?
    And who is a rock, save our God?
33 God is my strong fortress:
    And he guideth the perfect in his way.
34 He maketh his feet like hinds' *feet*:
    And setteth me upon my high places.
35 He teacheth my hands to war;
    So that mine arms do bend a bow of brass.
36 Thou hast also given me the shield of thy salvation:
    And thy gentleness hath made me great.
37 Thou hast enlarged my steps under me,
    And my feet have not slipped.

(*g*) *The great Overthrow.* 38-43.

38 I have pursued mine enemies, and destroyed them;
    Neither did I turn again till they were consumed.
39 And I have consumed them, and smitten them through,
        that they cannot arise:
    Yea, they are fallen under my feet.

---

30. I run upon (marg. 'through'). As at the charge at Baal-perazim (v. 20).
    I leap over a wall.   As at the storming of Jebus, the impregnable.
    36. thy gentleness.   David had imitated God's kindness in dealing with his foes; hence he had been made great by God's kindness.

For thou hast girded me with strength unto the battle : 40
Thou hast subdued under me those that rose up
    against me.
Thou hast also made mine enemies turn their backs 41
    unto me,
That I might cut off them that hate me.
They looked, but there was none to save ;   42
Even unto the LORD, but he answered them not.
Then did I beat them small as the dust of the earth, 43
I did stamp them as the mire of the streets, and did
    spread them abroad.

(*h*) *Supremacy granted to David.* 44-46.

Thou also hast delivered me from the strivings of my 44
    people ;
Thou hast kept me to be the head of the nations :
A people whom I have not known shall serve me.
The strangers shall submit themselves unto me :   45
As soon as they hear of me, they shall obey me.
The strangers shall fade away,   46
And shall come trembling out of their close places.

(*i*) *Recapitulation.* 47-51.

The LORD liveth ; and blessed be my rock ;   47
And exalted be the God of the rock of my salvation:

---

42. Even unto the Lord. This can refer only to Israelite
foes, who acknowledged Jehovah. He refused (e.g.) to answer
Saul (1 Sam. xxviii. 6).
44. the strivings of my people. Civil war with Ishbosheth.
Israel was now one united kingdom.
the head of the nations. The supremacy he had wrested
from Philistia. See note on viii. 1.
A people whom I have not known. May refer to some of the
distant people, beyond Lebanon and the Euphrates (viii. 3-10)
and Hiram of Tyre (v. 11 f.).
45. As soon as they hear. As Toi of Hamath (viii. 9 f.).
It may refer also to the many foreigners who served David in
civil and military posts.

48   Even the God that executeth vengeance for me,
      And bringeth down peoples under me,
49   And that bringeth me forth from mine enemies:
      Yea, thou liftest me up above them that rise up
            against me:
      Thou deliverest me from the violent man.
50   Therefore I will give thanks unto thee, O LORD,
            among the nations,
      And will sing praises unto thy name.
51   Great deliverance giveth he to his king:
      And sheweth lovingkindness to his anointed,
      To David and to his seed, for evermore.

xxiii. 1-7.   *David's Last Words.*

23   Now these be the last words of David.
      David the son of Jesse saith,
      And the man who was raised on high saith,
      The anointed of the God of Jacob,
      And the sweet psalmist of Israel:
2   The spirit of the LORD spake by me,
      And his word was upon my tongue.
3   The God of Israel said,
      The Rock of Israel spake to me:
      One that ruleth over men righteously,
      That ruleth in the fear of God,

---

49. the violent man. The representatives of the old policy
of force and revenge (Saul, Joab, Shimei &c.).

50. among the nations. Jebusites, Philistines and other
heathen may have listened to these solemn strains.

51. and to his seed. Cf. vii. 11-16.

xxiii. 1. last words. The 'last words' of a hero were a
recognised form of Hebrew poetical composition. It was sometimes called the 'Blessing.' Cf. Gen. xlix. 28 (Jacob) and
Deut. xxxiii. 1 (Moses).

2. The spirit of the Lord. A claim to inspiration. The
poem is an oracle.

3. The text of the poem is very corrupt. The burden is,

He shall be as the light of the morning, when the sun 4
    riseth,
A morning without clouds;
When the tender grass *springeth* out of the earth,
Through clear shining after rain.
Verily my house is not so with God;   5
Yet he hath made with me an everlasting covenant,
Ordered in all things, and sure:
For it is all my salvation, and all *my* desire,
Although he maketh it not to grow.
But the ungodly shall be all of them as thorns to be 6
    thrust away,
For they cannot be taken with the hand:
But the man that toucheth them   7
Must be armed with iron and the staff of a spear;
And they shall be utterly burned with fire in *their*
    place.

8–39.   *A List of Heroes and their Deeds.*

(a)   *The Three.*   8–12.

These be the names of the mighty men whom David 8
had: Josheb-basshebeth a Tahchemonite, chief of the
captains; the same was Adino the Eznite, against eight
hundred slain at one time.   And after him was Eleazar 9

---

that kings must rule by the Fear and Will of Jehovah.   Then
shall their rule be blessed.

5.   Read, with marg., 'For is not my house so with God?
for he   for all my salvation, and all my desire, will he not make
it to grow?'   David's testimony is that Jehovah for his righteousness has made firm his throne and dynasty.

6. ungodly. 'Men of Belial' (marg.), see note on xvi. 7.   The
violent, caring not for Jehovah's ways, shall perish by violence.

8. Josheb-basshebeth the Tahchemonite. A corruption probably for 'Ishbosheth the Hachmonite.'   The rest of the verse
is unintelligible.   It may mean 'he wielded his spear against
eight hundred,' as in 1 Chron. xi. 11.

the son of Dodai the son of an Ahohite, one of the three
mighty men with David, when they defied the Philistines
that were there gathered together to battle, and the men
10 of Israel were gone away: he arose, and smote the
Philistines until his hand was weary, and his hand clave
unto the sword: and the LORD wrought a great victory
that day ; and the people returned after him only to spoil.
11 And after him was Shammah the son of Agee a Hararite.
And the Philistines were gathered together into a troop,
where was a plot of ground full of lentils; and the people
12 fled from the Philistines.   But he stood in the midst of
the plot, and defended it, and slew the Philistines: and
the LORD wrought a great victory.

(b)   *The Exploit of the Water of Bethlehem.*   13-17.

13 And three of the thirty chief went down, and came to David
in the harvest time unto the cave of Adullam ; and the troop
of the Philistines were encamped in the valley of Rephaim.
14 And David was then in the hold, and the garrison of the
15 Philistines was then in Beth-lehem.   And David longed,
and said, Oh that one would give me water to drink of
16 the well of Beth-lehem, which is by the gate! And the
three mighty men brake through the host of the Philistines,
and drew water out of the well of Beth-lehem, that was by
the gate, and took it, and brought it to David: but he
would not drink thereof, but poured it out unto the LORD.
17 And he said, Be it far from me, O LORD, that I should do

---

9.   the three.   These three champions seem to have
formed an order by themselves.

13.   the thirty.   A second Order.

14.   And David &c.   It was probably in the first Philistine
war, David being entrenched at Adullam and the Philistines in
Rephaim (see v. 17 ff.).

16.   he would not drink.   David's appreciation of the deed
was worthy of the devotion of his men.   He felt it was their
life-blood they were offering him, and blood, the life, could only
be offered to Jehovah.

this: *shall I drink* the blood of the men that went in jeopardy of their lives? therefore he would not drink it. These things did the three mighty men.

(*c*) *Achievements of Abishai and Benaiah.* 18–23.

And Abishai, the brother of Joab, the son of Zeruiah, was 18 chief of the three.   And he lifted up his spear against three hundred and slew them, and had a name among the three. Was he not most honourable of the three? therefore he was 19 made their captain: howbeit he attained not unto the *first* three.   And Benaiah the son of Jehoiada, the son of a 20 valiant man of Kabzeel, who had done mighty deeds, he slew the two *sons of* Ariel of Moab: he went down also and slew a lion in the midst of a pit in time of snow: and 21 he slew an Egyptian, a goodly man: and the Egyptian had a spear in his hand; but he went down to him with a staff, and plucked the spear out of the Egyptian's hand, and slew him with his own spear.   These things did 22 Benaiah the son of Jehoiada, and had a name among the three mighty men.   He was more honourable than the 23 thirty, but he attained not to the *first* three.   And David set him over his guard.

(*d*) *The Roll of the Thirty.* 24–39.

Asahel the brother of Joab was one of the thirty; 24 Elhanan the son of Dodo of Beth-lehem; Shammah the 25

---

18. **chief of the three.** Read, 'thirty' for 'three'; the numbers in Hebrew are easily confused. He was the head of the second Order.

a name among the three. Read, 'thirty.'

19. **the three.** Read, 'the thirty.' **the first three.** Omit (also in *v.* 23) 'first,' which is not in the Heb.

20. **Benaiah.** Captain of David's guard (viii. 18 &c.).

22. **the three.** Read, 'the thirty.'

23. Abishai and Benaiah were distinguished among the Thirty, but for some reason were never promoted to the Three.

24. Asahel. As he was killed at the battle of Gibeon, this **Order** was in existence very early in David's reign.

26 Harodite, Elika the Harodite; Helez the Paltite, Ira the
27 son of Ikkesh the Tekoite; Abiezer the Anathothite,
28 Mebunnai the Hushathite; Zalmon the Ahohite, Maharai
29 the Netophathite; Heleb the son of Baanah the Netophathite, Ittai the son of Ribai of Gibeah of the children
30 of Benjamin; Benaiah a Pirathonite, Hiddai of the brooks
31 of Gaash; Abi-albon the Arbathite, Azmaveth the Bar-
32 humite; Eliahba the Shaalbonite, the sons of Jashen,
33 Jonathan; Shammah the Hararite, Ahiam the son of
34 Sharar the Ararite; Eliphelet the son of Ahasbai, the
son of the Maacathite, Eliam the son of Ahithophel the
35/36 Gilonite; Hezro the Carmelite, Paarai the Arbite; Igal
37 the son of Nathan of Zobah, Bani the Gadite; Zelek the
Ammonite, Naharai the Beerothite, armourbearers to
38 Joab the son of Zeruiah; Ira the Ithrite, Gareb the
39 Ithrite; Uriah the Hittite: thirty and seven in all.

xxiv. 1-9. *The unholy Enrolment.*

24   And again the anger of the LORD was kindled against
Israel, and he moved David against them, saying, Go,
2 number Israel and Judah.   And the king said to Joab

---

39. thirty and seven. As heroes fell, their vacant places
were filled up. Hence there are more than thirty members
named as belonging to this Order.

xxiv. 1. And again. Another extract from what we may call
'the Temple book of Precedents' (see note on xxi. 1).

the anger of the Lord. Shewn by the disastrous suggestion which followed, or by some national punishment not
recorded.

he moved. According to the later and truer idea of God it
was impossible to think of Him as inciting His people to sin;
the Chronicler therefore (1 Chr. xxi. 1) substituted: 'Satan stood
up against Israel and moved David &c.' Satan is the adversary
of God's people, whose work is to tempt them to their destruction.

Go, number. i.e. 'enrol.' Apparently in a time of peace the
scheme was suggested to David of strengthening his military

the captain of the host, which was with him, Go now to
and fro through all the tribes of Israel, from Dan even to
Beer-sheba, and number ye the people, that I may know
the sum of the people. And Joab said unto the king, 3
Now the LORD thy God add unto the people, how many
soever they be, an hundredfold, and may the eyes of my
lord the king see it: but why doth my lord the king
delight in this thing? Notwithstanding the king's word 4
prevailed against Joab, and against the captains of the
host. And Joab and the captains of the host went out
from the presence of the king, to number the people of
Israel. And they passed over Jordan, and pitched in 5
Aroer, on the right side of the city that is in the middle
of the valley of Gad, and unto Jazer: then they came to 6

---

resources by raising a standing army consisting of the whole
population available for military service. But war being the
service of Jehovah (see note on i. 12) the army was only enrolled
when actually required. They could not, when enrolled, go
about their ordinary duties. If however the nation formed a
standing army, it would be impossible to regard that state of life
as consecrated, i.e. separated and exceptional, which had become
continuous and general. Hence war would cease to be a holy
thing, and would come to be waged at the will of kings, instead
of at Jehovah's bidding. This then, the classic instance of an
attempt to raise a standing army in Israel, was condemned by
a signal declaration of Jehovah's displeasure. There is probably
a reference to this incident in Ex. xxx. 12.

2. to Joab. That Joab was entrusted with this mission
shews that it was a military measure. He was to prepare a
register of all males of age for military service.

3. And Joab said. This was a novelty and an encroachment
upon the free independence of Israel, and therefore distasteful to
Joab and the conservatives.

4. the king's word prevailed. Israel was bitten with
militarism; David merely voiced popular sentiment. Hence the
people were involved in the Divine anger.

5 ff. The enumerators began with Eastern Israel, working from
south to north, then westward under Mount Hermon to the coast
at Zidon, then down through Western Palestine to the extreme
south The Chronicler adds that Levi and Benjamin were
omitted (1 Chron. xxi. 6).

Gilead, and to the land of Tahtim-hodshi; and they came
7 to Dan-jaan, and round about to Zidon, and came to the
strong hold of Tyre, and to all the cities of the Hivites,
and of the Canaanites: and they went out to the south of
8 Judah, at Beer-sheba. So when they had gone to and fro
through all the land, they came to Jerusalem at the end of
9 nine months and twenty days. And Joab gave up the
sum of the numbering of the people unto the king: and
there were in Israel eight hundred thousand valiant men
that drew the sword; and the men of Judah were five
hundred thousand men.

10–14. *The Choice of Punishment.*

10 And David's heart smote him after that he had numbered
the people. And David said unto the LORD, I have sinned
greatly in that I have done: but now, O LORD, put away,
I beseech thee, the iniquity of thy servant ; for I have done
11 very foolishly. And when David rose up in the morning,
the word of the LORD came unto the prophet Gad, David's
12 seer, saying, Go and speak unto David, Thus saith the
LORD, I offer thee three things; choose thee one of them,
13 that I may do it unto thee. So Gad came to David, and
told him, and said unto him, Shall seven years of famine
come unto thee in thy land? or wilt thou flee three months
before thy foes while they pursue thee? or shall there be
three days' pestilence in thy land? now advise thee, and
consider what answer I shall return to him that sent me.
14 And David said unto Gad, I am in a great strait: let us
fall now into the hand of the LORD; for his mercies are
great: and let me not fall into the hand of man.

---

11. Gad. One of David's followers in exile (1 Sam. xxii. 5).
13. seven years. The Chronicler (as LXX here) reads, 'three years,' answering to 'three months' and 'three days.'
14. his mercies are great. One of David's strongest convictions was that God's justice is tempered with mercy.

15–17. *The Plague.*

So the LORD sent a pestilence upon Israel from the 15
morning even to the time appointed: and there died of
the people from Dan even to Beer-sheba seventy thousand
men. And when the angel stretched out his hand toward 16
Jerusalem to destroy it, the LORD repented him of the
evil, and said to the angel that destroyed the people, It is
enough; now stay thine hand. And the angel of the
LORD was by the threshing-floor of Araunah the Jebusite.
And David spake unto the LORD when he saw the angel 17
that smote the people, and said, Lo, I have sinned, and I
have done perversely: but these sheep, what have they
done? let thine hand, I pray thee, be against me, and
against my father's house.

18–25. *The Altar at Araunah's Threshing-Floor.*

And Gad came that day to David, and said unto him, 18
Go up, rear an altar unto the LORD in the threshing-floor

---

15. even to the time appointed. Must mean, till the end
of the third day. But before that time the plague was stopped
at David's intercession. The LXX gives a better sense : 'And
David chose the pestilence; and it was the days of wheat harvest
(corroborated by 1 Chron. xxi. 20); and the Lord dealt death in
Israel from early morning till the hour of mid-day; and the
plague began among the people, and there died &c.'

16. the Lord repented. His actions are those of a Person,
not of a mere Force. He is moved by His own goodness and by
man's prayers. His repentance is not sorrow for doing wrong,
but a change of mind, here from anger to pity, punishment having
gone far enough. He is thought of as having a special tenderness
for Jerusalem.

the threshing-floor of Araunah. A further reason for the
inclusion of this account is that it gives ' the charter of the most
famous of the world's holy places' (Kennedy). Upon this rock,
thus sanctified, Solomon's altar was reared (see on *v.* 25); and to
this day it is revered by Jews, Christians and Mohammedans.

17. I have sinned &c. Two signs of real penitence are
willingness to bear pain and tender pity for others.

19 of Araunah the Jebusite. And David went up according
20 to the saying of Gad, as the LORD commanded. And
Araunah looked forth, and saw the king and his servants
coming on toward him: and Araunah went out, and bowed
21 himself before the king with his face to the ground. And
Araunah said, Wherefore is my lord the king come to his
servant? And David said, To buy the threshing-floor of
thee, to build an altar unto the LORD, that the plague may
22 be stayed from the people. And Araunah said unto David,
Let my lord the king take and offer up what seemeth good
unto him : behold, the oxen for the burnt offering, and the
threshing instruments and the furniture of the oxen for the
23 wood: all this, O king, doth Araunah give unto the king.
And Araunah said unto the king, The LORD thy God
24 accept thee. And the king said unto Araunah, Nay; but
I will verily buy it of thee at a price : neither will I offer
burnt offerings unto the LORD my God which cost me
nothing. So David bought the threshing-floor and the
25 oxen for fifty shekels of silver. And David built there
an altar unto the LORD, and offered burnt offerings and
peace offerings. So the LORD was intreated for the land,
and the plague was stayed from Israel.

---

18. Araunah. One of the original non-Israelite inhabitants
of Jerusalem. He may have been king (marg.).

22 f. An instance of Oriental courtesy.

24. neither will I offer &c. The true spirit of sacrifice.

fifty shekels. About £7 of our money, but in actual value
equal to much more.

25. David built there an altar. Identified by later writers
with the site of Solomon's Temple. Cf. 1 Chron. xxii. 1 and
2 Chron. iii. 1.

INDEX

For EU product safety concerns, contact us at Calle de José Abascal, 56–1°, 28003 Madrid, Spain or eugpsr@cambridge.org.

www.ingramcontent.com/pod-product-compliance
Ingram Content Group UK Ltd.
Pitfield, Milton Keynes, MK11 3LW, UK
UKHW020311140625
459647UK00018B/1828